Cooking Light

200-CALORIE

recipes · hints · tips

Oxmoor House

Welcome

It's no secret—fad diets come and go. But for *Cooking Light*, the secret to healthful eating is super simple: eat sensibly. And to that end, one of the best things you can do is count calories. Not only does counting calories assist in weight loss, but it's an integral component of weight maintenance, too.

Let *Cooking Light Eat Smart Guide: 200-Calorie* be your go-to source for choosing calories wisely. With more than 80 delicious, easy, and filling recipes, this book shows you specifically how you can make eating an enjoyable experience once again, even while counting calories.

Each recipe in this handy guidebook comes in under 200 calories, and you'll find a wide range of recipes for whatever you're craving. From appetizers, snacks, and beverages to main course dishes and everything in between—there's something here just for you.

Every recipe has been carefully tested to ensure quality and satisfaction. In addition, each recipe comes with a complete nutritional analysis to help you make savvy choices that suit your lifestyle. Choose from mouthwatering dishes such as Balsamic Chicken and Mushrooms (150 calories, page 66), Taco Salad with Cilantro-Lime Vinaigrette (198 calories, page 75), and Triple-Chocolate Pudding (169 calories, page 140).

But it's not just about recipes! *Cooking Light Eat Smart Guide: 200-Calorie* also offers helpful ideas and tips for staying on the healthy bandwagon. Special features include "Snacking Strategies" (page 30), "8 Top Secrets of Portion Control" (page 50), and "How to Make Great Low-Fat Cookies" (page 154). Combine these great resources with the delicious, easy-to-make recipes, and you're well on your way to the ultimate goal—making healthy taste great.

The *Cooking Light* Editors

ISBN-10: 0-8487-3438-6
ISBN-13: 978-0-8487-3438-1
Library of Congress Control Number: 2010933257

Printed in the United States of America
First Printing 2011

OXMOOR HOUSE

VP, Publishing Director: Jim Childs
Editorial Director: Susan Payne Dobbs
Brand Manager: Michelle Turner Aycock
Senior Editor: Heather Averett
Managing Editor: Laurie S. Herr

Cooking Light Eat Smart Guide: 200-Calorie

Editor: Andrea C. Kirkland, MS, RD
Project Editor: Emily Chappell
Senior Designer: Emily Albright Parrish
Assistant Designer: Allison L. Sperando
Director, Test Kitchens: Elizabeth Tyler Austin
Assistant Directors, Test Kitchens:
    Julie Christopher, Julie Gunter
Test Kitchens Professionals: Wendy Ball,
    Allison E. Cox, Victoria E. Cox,
    Margaret Monroe Dickey,
    Alyson Moreland Haynes, Callie Nash,
    Kathleen Royal Phillips, Catherine Crowell Steele,
    Leah Van Deren
Photography Director: Jim Bathie
Senior Photo Stylist: Kay E. Clarke
Associate Photo Stylist: Katherine Eckert Coyne
Assistant Photo Stylist: Mary Louise Menendez
Senior Production Manager: Greg A. Amason

Contributors

Copy Editor: Norma Butterworth-McKittrick
Proofreader: Lauren Brooks
Interns: Christine T. Boatwright, Caitlin Watzke
Test Kitchens Professional: Elizabeth Nelson

Cooking Light.

Editor: Scott Mowbray
Creative Director: Carla Frank
Deputy Editor: Phillip Rhodes
Food Editor: Ann Taylor Pittman
Special Publications Editor:
    Mary Simpson Creel, MS, RD
Associate Food Editors: Timothy Q. Cebula,
    Julianna Grimes
Associate Editors: Cindy Hatcher, Brandy Rushing
Test Kitchens Director: Vanessa T. Pruett
Assistant Test Kitchens Director:
    Tiffany Vickers Davis
Chief Food Stylist: Charlotte Autry
Senior Food Stylist: Kellie Gerber Kelley
Recipe Testers and Developers: Robin Bashinsky,
    Adam Hickman, Deb Wise
Art Director: Fernande Bondarenko
Junior Deputy Art Director: Alexander Spacher
Associate Art Director: Rachel Lasserre
Designer: Chase Turberville
Photo Director: Kristen Schaefer
Senior Photographer: Randy Mayor
Senior Photo Stylist: Cindy Barr
Photo Stylist: Leigh Ann Ross
Copy Chief: Maria Parker Hopkins
Assistant Copy Chief: Susan Roberts
Research Editor: Michelle Gibson Daniels
Editorial Production Director: Liz Rhoades
Production Editor: Hazel R. Eddins
Art/Production Assistant: Josh Rutledge
Administrative Coordinator: Carol D. Johnson
CookingLight.com Editor: Allison Long Lowery
Nutrition Editor: Holley Johnson Grainger, MS, RD
Production Assistant: Mallory Daugherty

To order additional publications, call 1-800-765-6400 or 1-800-491-0551.
For more books to enrich your life, visit
oxmoorhouse.com
To search, savor, and share thousands of recipes, visit
myrecipes.com

Contents

Appetizers, Snacks & Beverages

QUICK&EASY

Sliders with Shallot-Dijon Relish

These mini-burgers make fun and tasty appetizers. Although we enjoyed them on Parker House rolls, they would also be tasty on small dinner rolls or sweet Hawaiian bread rolls.

$1/2$ teaspoon kosher salt
$1/4$ teaspoon freshly ground black pepper
1 pound ground sirloin
Cooking spray
3 tablespoons finely chopped shallots

1 tablespoon Worcestershire sauce
1 tablespoon Dijon mustard
2 teaspoons butter, softened
8 (1-ounce) Parker House rolls
16 dill pickle chips

1. Prepare grill to medium-high heat.
2. Combine salt, pepper, and sirloin. Divide meat mixture into 8 equal portions, shaping each into a $1/4$-inch-thick patty. Lightly coat both sides of patties with cooking spray. Place patties on grill rack; grill 3 minutes on each side or until done.
3. Combine shallots, Worcestershire sauce, mustard, and butter in a small bowl, stirring well. Cut rolls in half horizontally. Spread shallot mixture evenly over cut sides of rolls. Layer 1 patty and 2 pickle chips on bottom half of each roll; top with top halves of rolls. YIELD: 8 servings (serving size: 1 slider).

CALORIES 167; FAT 6.8g (sat 2.6g, mono 2.7g, poly 0.8g); PROTEIN 10.8g; CARB 14.2g; FIBER 1g; CHOL 23mg; IRON 1.8mg; SODIUM 404mg; CALC 7mg

167
calories

9

MAKE AHEAD

Fig and Goat Cheese Bruschetta

Prepare the fig jam up to three days in advance, and store it in the refrigerator. Bring it to room temperature, and assemble the bruschetta just before serving. For smaller groups, use half the amount of bread. Leftover jam is great on toast at breakfast.

1¼ cups chopped dried Mission figs (about 9 ounces)

⅓ cup sugar

⅓ cup coarsely chopped orange sections

1 teaspoon grated orange rind

⅓ cup fresh orange juice (about 1 orange)

½ teaspoon chopped fresh rosemary

¼ teaspoon freshly ground black pepper

40 (½-inch-thick) slices French bread baguette, toasted (about 8 ounces)

1¼ cups (10 ounces) crumbled goat cheese

5 teaspoons finely chopped walnuts

1. Preheat oven to 350°.

2. Combine first 7 ingredients in a small saucepan; bring to a boil. Cover, reduce heat, and simmer 10 minutes or until figs are tender. Uncover and cook 5 minutes or until mixture thickens. Remove from heat; cool to room temperature.

3. Preheat broiler.

4. Top each bread slice with 1½ teaspoons fig mixture and 1½ teaspoons goat cheese. Arrange bruschetta on a baking sheet; sprinkle evenly with walnuts. Broil 2 minutes or until nuts begin to brown. Serve warm. YIELD: 20 servings (serving size: 2 bruschetta).

CALORIES 138; FAT 4.7g (sat 2.3g, mono 1.1g, poly 1g); PROTEIN 4.2g; CARB 21g; FIBER 2.1g; CHOL 7mg; IRON 0.8mg; SODIUM 121mg; CALC 45mg

CHOICE INGREDIENT: *Rosemary*

Rosemary is one of the most aromatic and pungent of all herbs. Its needlelike leaves have a pronounced lemon-pine flavor that pairs well with olive and garlic. Rosemary is also a nice addition to sweet and savory dishes, but because its flavor is strong, use a light hand.

138 calories

61 calories

Prosciutto-Melon Bites with Lime Drizzle

16 (1-inch) cubes cantaloupe

16 (1-inch) cubes honeydew melon

16 (¼-ounce) very thin slices prosciutto, cut in half lengthwise

1 tablespoon fresh lime juice

2 teaspoons extra-virgin olive oil

¼ teaspoon crushed red pepper

2 tablespoons thinly sliced fresh mint

1. Wrap each cantaloupe cube and each honeydew cube with ½ prosciutto slice. Thread 1 wrapped cantaloupe cube and 1 wrapped honeydew cube onto each of 16 (4-inch) skewers. Arrange skewers on a serving platter.

2. Combine lime juice, oil, and pepper, stirring with a whisk; drizzle evenly over skewers. Sprinkle evenly with mint. YIELD: 8 servings (serving size: 2 skewers).

CALORIES 61; FAT 3g (sat 0.8g, mono 1.7g, poly 0.5g); PROTEIN 4.2g; CARB 5g; FIBER 0.3g; CHOL 13mg; IRON 0.3mg; SODIUM 282mg; CALC 5mg

RECIPE BENEFIT: low-carb

CHOICE INGREDIENT: *Prosciutto*

Prosciutto (pro-SHOO-toh), also known as Parma ham, is a salt-cured ham that is typically sliced thin and often eaten raw or lightly cooked, making it perfect to use in quick-cooking recipes. A little prosciutto offers a powerful punch of flavor in this dish, so you'll only need to use a small amount.

84
calories

Grilled Pepper Poppers

The three-cheese filling is a nice complement for the spicy peppers. You can also use a milder chile, such as a cherry pepper. Shredded cheddar cheese can take the place of Parmesan, if you'd like.

½ cup (4 ounces) soft goat cheese
½ cup (4 ounces) fat-free cream cheese, softened
½ cup (2 ounces) grated fresh Parmesan cheese
½ cup finely chopped seeded tomato
2 tablespoons thinly sliced green onions
2 tablespoons chopped fresh sage
½ teaspoon kosher salt
16 jalapeño peppers, halved lengthwise and seeded (about 1½ pounds)
Cooking spray
2 tablespoons chopped fresh cilantro

1. Prepare grill to medium-high heat.

2. Combine first 7 ingredients in a bowl, stirring well. Spoon about 2 teaspoons cheese mixture into each pepper half. Place pepper halves, cheese side up, on grill rack coated with cooking spray. Grill peppers 5 minutes or until bottoms of peppers are charred and cheese mixture is lightly browned. Carefully place peppers on a serving platter. Sprinkle with cilantro. YIELD: 16 servings (serving size: 2 pepper halves).

CALORIES 84; FAT 4.8g (sat 3.1g, mono 1.2g, poly 0.2g); PROTEIN 7.1g; CARB 3.5g; FIBER 0.9g; CHOL 11mg; IRON 0.6mg; SODIUM 334mg; CALC 117mg

RECIPE BENEFIT: low-carb

Parmesan Zucchini Sticks with Smoky Roasted Romesco Sauce

Crunchy breaded zucchini spears are delicious dipped in a summery sauce of roasted red peppers. The sauce is a zesty embellishment for grilled meats, too.

3 medium red bell peppers

2 plum tomatoes, halved lengthwise

1/2 cup (1/2-inch) cubed French bread baguette, crusts removed

1 1/2 tablespoons smoked almonds

1 tablespoon extra-virgin olive oil

1 tablespoon sherry vinegar or red wine vinegar

1/4 teaspoon Spanish smoked paprika

1/4 teaspoon kosher salt

1/8 teaspoon ground red pepper

1 large garlic clove

3 large zucchini (about 1 1/2 pounds)

1 cup dry breadcrumbs

1/2 cup panko (Japanese breadcrumbs)

1/4 cup (1 ounce) grated fresh Parmesan cheese

1/2 teaspoon salt

1/2 teaspoon freshly ground black pepper

1/2 cup egg substitute

Cooking spray

1. Preheat broiler.

2. Cut bell peppers in half lengthwise; discard seeds and membranes. Place bell pepper halves and tomatoes, skin sides up, on a foil-lined baking sheet; flatten bell peppers with hand. Broil 10 minutes or until blackened. Place in a zip-top plastic bag; seal. Let stand 15 minutes. Peel and coarsely chop, reserving any liquid.

3. Combine bell peppers, reserved liquid, tomatoes, and next 8 ingredients in a blender or food processor; process until smooth.

4. Preheat oven to 400°.

5. Cut 1 zucchini in half crosswise; cut each half lengthwise into 8 wedges. Repeat procedure with remaining zucchini. Combine breadcrumbs, panko, cheese, 1/2 teaspoon salt, and black pepper in a shallow dish. Dip zucchini in egg substitute; dredge in breadcrumb mixture. Place zucchini on a wire rack coated with cooking spray. Lightly coat zucchini with cooking spray. Bake at 400° for 25 minutes or until golden brown. Serve immediately with sauce. YIELD: 8 servings (serving size: 6 zucchini sticks and 1/4 cup sauce).

CALORIES 170; FAT 5.6g (sat 1.3g, mono 2.5g, poly 1.3g); PROTEIN 8.4g; CARB 23.4g; FIBER 3.9g; CHOL 3mg; IRON 1.9mg; SODIUM 434mg; CALC 107mg

170 calories

Traditional Hummus

This Middle Eastern dip is traditionally made with chickpeas, tahini, lemon juice, and olive oil. Prepare and refrigerate it a day ahead; let it stand at room temperature for 30 minutes before serving.

44 calories

- 2 (15.5-ounce) cans no-salt-added chickpeas (garbanzo beans), rinsed and drained
- 2 garlic cloves, crushed
- ½ cup water
- ¼ cup tahini (sesame seed paste)
- 3 tablespoons fresh lemon juice
- 2 tablespoons extra-virgin olive oil
- ¾ teaspoon salt
- ¼ teaspoon black pepper

1. Place beans and garlic in a food processor; pulse 5 times or until chopped. Add ½ cup water and remaining ingredients; pulse until smooth, scraping down sides as needed. YIELD: 3¼ cups (serving size: 2 tablespoons).

CALORIES 44; FAT 2.5g (sat 0.3g, mono 1.2g, poly 0.7g); PROTEIN 1.5g; CARB 4.4g; FIBER 0.9g; CHOL 0mg; IRON 0.3mg; SODIUM 74mg; CALC 12mg

WHITE BEAN AND ROASTED GARLIC HUMMUS

Since this variation calls for roasted garlic, you can just omit the raw crushed garlic cloves from the Traditional Hummus. Remove white papery skin from 2 whole garlic heads (do not peel or separate the cloves). Wrap each head separately in foil. Bake at 350° for 1 hour; cool 10 minutes. Separate cloves; squeeze to extract garlic pulp. Discard skins. Place garlic pulp, Traditional Hummus, and 1 (15-ounce) can rinsed and drained cannellini beans (or other white beans) in a food processor; pulse 5 times or until chopped. Add ¼ cup water; process until smooth, scraping down sides as needed. Stir in ¾ teaspoon chopped fresh rosemary. YIELD: 5 cups (serving size: about 2½ tablespoons).

CALORIES 45; FAT 2g (sat 0.3g, mono 1g, poly 0.6g); PROTEIN 1.8g; CARB 5.3g; FIBER 1.2g; CHOL 0mg; IRON 0.4mg; SODIUM 81mg; CALC 16mg

SPICY RED PEPPER HUMMUS

Cut 2 red bell peppers in half lengthwise; discard seeds and membranes. Place pepper halves, skin sides up, on a foil-lined baking sheet; flatten with hand. Broil 15 minutes or until blackened. Place in a zip-top plastic bag; seal. Let stand 10 minutes. Peel and cut into strips. Combine bell peppers, 2 teaspoons chile paste with garlic (such as sambal oelek), ½ teaspoon paprika, and ⅛ teaspoon ground red pepper in a food processor; pulse until smooth. Transfer pepper mixture to a serving bowl; stir in Traditional Hummus. YIELD: 4 cups (serving size: about 2 tablespoons).

CALORIES 39; FAT 2g (sat 0.3g, mono 1g, poly 0.6g); PROTEIN 1.4g; CARB 4.3g; FIBER 1g; CHOL 0mg; IRON 0.3mg; SODIUM 74mg; CALC 11mg

take two:
Hummus vs. Salsa

Since salsa is made only of vegetables, it has fewer calories and grams of fat than dense, creamy hummus, which contains healthful fats from olive oil and tahini (sesame seed paste). But consider that you probably won't eat either unaccompanied. One serving of standard corn tortilla chips will add calories, fat grams, and sodium to salsa. Hummus, in contrast, is a natural partner for nutritious dippers like carrot and celery sticks.

Hummus
(2 tablespoons)
47 calories
3 grams fat
1 gram fiber
84 milligrams sodium

Carrot Sticks
(¼ cup)
13 calories
0 grams fat
21 milligrams sodium

Tomato Salsa
(2 tablespoons)
5 calories
0 grams fat
0.5 gram fiber
38 milligrams sodium

Tortilla Chips
(1 ounce)
142 calories
7 grams fat
149 milligrams sodium

Warm Caramelized Onion Dip

Serve with hearty crackers or slices of French bread.

81 calories

- **2** teaspoons olive oil
- **4** cups chopped onion (about 2 large onions)
- **¾** teaspoon chopped fresh thyme
- **½** cup light sour cream
- **⅓** cup (about 1½ ounces) grated Parmigiano-Reggiano cheese
- **⅓** cup (3 ounces) ⅓-less-fat cream cheese
- **⅓** cup reduced-fat mayonnaise
- **¼** teaspoon salt
- **¼** teaspoon freshly ground black pepper
- **¼** teaspoon hot pepper sauce (such as Tabasco)
- **¼** teaspoon Worcestershire sauce

1. Heat oil in a large nonstick skillet over medium-high heat, swirling to coat pan. Add chopped onion and thyme to pan; sauté 10 minutes or until golden brown. Reduce heat to low; cook 20 minutes or until onions are deep golden brown, stirring occasionally. Remove onion mixture from heat. Add sour cream and remaining ingredients, stirring until blended and cheese melts. YIELD: 12 servings (serving size: 3 tablespoons).

CALORIES 81; FAT 4.9g (sat 2.3g, mono 1.2g, poly 0.6g); PROTEIN 3.1g; CARB 7.7g; FIBER 0.9g; CHOL 12mg; IRON 0mg; SODIUM 206mg; CALC 58mg

INGREDIENT TIP: Ground black pepper packed in a tin or a jar is convenient, but it lacks the natural oil that helps give the spice its bite. Grinding whole fresh peppercorns just before you need them releases their oils, resulting in a more vivid flavor that is key to adding a bit of kick to creamy dips like this. In our experience, 10 full cranks of a pepper mill produces about a ¼ teaspoon of coarsely ground pepper.

5 Healthy Office Snacks

Research shows that eating every four hours helps keep your metabolism charged and your energy level high. Plan ahead, and stash low-calorie, nutritious snacks in your briefcase, purse, or desk. Each of these sure-to-satisfy snacks has less than 200 calories.

1. Whole-Wheat Crackers and Peanut Butter

FOR A HUNGER-CURBING OPTION, pack 10 multigrain wheat crackers and a tablespoon of peanut butter. This nutrient-rich snack rings in at just 193 calories and offers 2 grams of fiber. The combination of complex carbs and protein will help keep your blood sugar stable and you feeling full longer.

2. Fruit

GRAB AN APPLE, BANANA, PEAR, GRAPES, OR OTHER PORTABLE FRUIT AS YOU DASH OUT THE DOOR EVERY MORNING. If you grab a different fruit every day (and change with the seasons), you'll obtain a good variety of nutrients plus fiber, and you won't get bored with the same old snack. The average serving of fruit is around 70 calories so pair it with a cup of fat-free milk (about 90 calories) for a protein boost as well as extra calcium and vitamin D. This protein and fiber combination will keep you feeling full and prevent mindless eating.

3. Popcorn with Parmesan

TAKE REGULAR BAGGED POPCORN TO THE NEXT LEVEL BY TOPPING IT WITH 2 TABLESPOONS OF SHREDDED PARMESAN CHEESE. The nutty flavor of the popcorn pairs well with the rich flavor of Parmesan, resulting in a quick, 150-calorie snack. Simply top 3½ cups of 94%-fat-free popcorn with the cheese, and your snack is ready. If you don't have an office fridge to stash your Parm, nosh on just the popcorn for only 100 calories. This salty snack counts as one of your three daily servings of whole grains and helps increase your energy and improve your mood.

4. Nuts

MAKE THE SWAP, AND CHOOSE NUTS OVER CHIPS FOR A CRUNCHY ALTERNATIVE. Nuts are rich in heart-healthy fats, but they are calorically dense (about 170 calories per ounce) so measure out an ounce (about 24 almonds), and stick to that amount instead of feasting on the entire bag. Store premeasured baggies of nuts in an office drawer or your purse to nibble on when the 3 p.m. hunger pains hit. Almonds and other nuts are a naturally high source of vitamin E, calcium, magnesium, and potassium, and they are rich in protein and fiber.

5. Veggies with Hummus

BEAT HIGH-FAT, HIGH-SODIUM SNACKS BY PACKING A CONTAINER OF FRESH VEGGIES LIKE CARROTS, CELERY, AND GRAPE TOMATOES. Raw veggies fill you up because of their high water and fiber content. If you struggle eating veggies in the buff, try dipping them in 2 tablespoons of hummus (60 calories).

Creamy Garlic-Herb Dip

You can prepare this all-purpose dip up to a day ahead. Serve it with cauliflower and broccoli florets, carrot and celery sticks, and bell pepper strips.

½ cup (4 ounces) ⅓-less-fat cream cheese	1 teaspoon grated lemon rind
¼ cup buttermilk	¼ teaspoon salt
2 tablespoons minced fresh chives	⅛ teaspoon freshly ground black pepper
1 tablespoon minced fresh parsley	1 small garlic clove, minced

1. Combine all ingredients in a bowl; beat with a mixer at high speed for 2 minutes or until smooth. YIELD: ¾ cup (serving size: 2 tablespoons).

CALORIES 55; FAT 4.4g (sat 2.9g, mono 1.3g, poly 0.1g); PROTEIN 2.5g; CARB 1.5g; FIBER 0.1g; CHOL 15mg; IRON 0.1mg; SODIUM 195mg; CALC 17mg

RECIPE BENEFIT: low-carb

KITCHEN TIP: A Microplane® food grater is the ideal tool to use when a recipe calls for grated lemon rind or lemon zest. It's fast and efficient, and it removes only the intensely flavored yellow lemon rind without any of the white pith, which is very bitter.

55
calories

98 calories

Chili-Spiced Almonds

These flavorful nuts make a convenient, portable snack. Store them at room temperature in an airtight container for up to a week.

1 tablespoon water
1 large egg white
1 pound raw, unblanched almonds
½ cup sugar
1 tablespoon salt

1 teaspoon Spanish smoked paprika
1 teaspoon ground cumin
1 teaspoon ground coriander
½ teaspoon chili powder
Cooking spray

1. Preheat oven to 300°.

2. Combine 1 tablespoon water and egg white in a large bowl; stir with a whisk until foamy. Add almonds; toss well to coat. Place almonds in a colander, and drain 5 minutes.

3. Combine coated almonds, sugar, and next 5 ingredients in a large bowl; toss to coat. Spread almond mixture in a single layer on a jelly-roll pan coated with cooking spray. Bake at 300° for 15 minutes. Stir almond mixture; reduce oven temperature to 275°. Bake an additional 40 minutes, stirring every 10 minutes. Remove from oven; cool 5 minutes. Break apart any clusters. Cool completely. YIELD: 4 cups (serving size: 2 tablespoons).

CALORIES 98; FAT 7.2g (sat 0.5g, mono 4.5g, poly 1.6g); PROTEIN 3.1g; CARB 6g; FIBER 1.8g; CHOL 0mg; IRON 0mg; SODIUM 221mg; CALC 1mg

91
calories

Orange Chipotle-Spiced Pecan Mix

Prepare a batch of this smoky-sweet mix to have on hand when visitors drop by. Or pack them into handsome jars to give as gifts. Store in an airtight container for up to one week.

- 1 tablespoon grated orange rind
- 1 tablespoon fresh orange juice
- 1 large egg white
- 2 cups pecan halves
- 1 tablespoon dark brown sugar
- 1 teaspoon kosher salt
- ½ teaspoon ground chipotle chile pepper
- Cooking spray
- ½ cup sweetened dried cranberries

1. Preheat oven to 225°.

2. Combine first 3 ingredients in a medium bowl; stir with a whisk. Stir in pecans. Combine sugar, salt, and pepper. Add to pecan mixture; toss well. Spread mixture in a single layer on a jelly-roll pan coated with cooking spray. Bake at 225° for 1 hour, stirring occasionally. Remove from oven; cool completely. Stir in cranberries. YIELD: 2½ cups (serving size: 2 tablespoons).

CALORIES 91; FAT 7.7g (sat 0.7g, mono 4.6g, poly 2.4g); PROTEIN 1.2g; CARB 4.8g; FIBER 0.8g; CHOL 0mg; IRON 0.3mg; SODIUM 98mg; CALC 1mg

RECIPE BENEFIT: low-carb

CHOICE INGREDIENT: *Cranberries*

Whether fresh, dried, cooked, or made into juice, cranberries are full of health benefits. They contain tannins, which help prevent infection. Tannins are also antioxidants, which neutralize harmful free radicals. Plus, cranberries have a high vitamin-C content. Dried cranberries are a terrific snack and a tasty addition to this pecan mix.

Snacking Strategies

Here are four situations where eating between meals can work for you:

1. If your energy levels are flagging.

SOLUTION: Consuming caffeine—in the form of coffee or tea—can help boost energy and alertness. Adding a bit of sugar and low-fat milk—if you prefer—only adds about 50 calories. Eating foods that blend complex carbohydrates and lean protein can also provide energy. Complex carbohydrates provide readily available fuel for your body, while protein increases the brain's dopamine levels, thereby boosting alertness. Healthful choices include a small handful of dried fruit and nuts, whole-grain crackers with a slice of cheese or a hard-boiled egg, or yogurt topped with a tablespoon of granola.

2. If mealtime is several hours away, but you're hungry now.

SOLUTION: For a snack with staying power, eat something that mixes fiber and protein. This is also a good strategy to tide you over until morning if you become hungry before bedtime. In a study at Wayne State University in Detroit, researchers found that when nighttime snackers developed the habit of eating cereal with milk 90 minutes after dinner, they reduced their total daily calorie intake and increased their chances of losing weight, compared to those who ate whatever they wanted. The cereal's fiber and protein combination kept them full—and prevented less mindful eating that can accompany evening routines. Other good hunger-curbing pairings include carrot sticks with hummus or black bean dip or a slice of multigrain bread spread with a tablespoon of reduced-fat peanut butter.

3. If you need a pre- or post-workout pick-me-up.

SOLUTION: Before a workout, consuming complex carbohydrates—such as fruit or whole-grain cereal—will provide your body with energy for exercise. Afterward, eat high-quality protein, such as low-fat yogurt or whole-grain cereal—particularly if you performed resistance exercises. A weight workout will stimulate the growth of muscle cells, which depend on protein. And, as always, consume plenty of fluids before, during, and after exercising.

4. If a stressful situation makes you feel an irrepressible urge to munch.

SOLUTION: In this instance, your desire for food may be hard-wired. Research from the University of California, San Francisco, found that consuming food—particularly items that contain sugar and fat—appears to calm the body's hormonal response to stress. But before you head to the vending machine, take a series of deep breaths; delay reaching for food for 15 minutes; drink a hot beverage such as tea, which can be soothing; and distract yourself by calling a friend or taking a walk. If you still feel like eating, then you're probably hungry. Eat a smart snack that fits your craving—a small piece of chocolate with a glass of skim milk, for example.

Mango Lassi

Choose low-fat or fat-free dairy products to keep saturated fat in check while delivering healthful calcium, potassium, and vitamin D. This sweet Indian-style, smoothie-like drink is a blend of fresh mango, tangy plain yogurt, and milk.

137 calories

1 cup chopped fresh mango	½ cup 1% low-fat milk
1½ tablespoons sugar	2 teaspoons chopped pistachios
1½ cups plain fat-free Greek yogurt	Dash of ground cardamom (optional)

1. Combine mango and sugar in a blender; process until pureed. Add yogurt and milk; process until smooth. Serve with pistachios; sprinkle with cardamom, if desired. YIELD: 3 servings (serving size: 1 cup lassi and about ½ teaspoon pistachios).

CALORIES 137; FAT 1.4g (sat 0.4g, mono 0.6g, poly 0.3g); PROTEIN 7g; CARB 27.5g; FIBER 1.2g; CHOL 4mg; IRON 0.2mg; SODIUM 89mg; CALC 207mg

RECIPE BENEFITS: low-fat; low-sodium

Blueberry Power Smoothie

With plenty of fruit, fiber, and protein, this quick shake is a sweet snack you can feel good about. You can also enjoy a larger serving as a healthful breakfast.

200 calories

1 cup fresh or frozen blueberries	2 tablespoons raspberry spread (such as Polaner All Fruit)
⅔ cup fat-free milk	1 (6-ounce) carton raspberry low-fat yogurt
½ cup reduced-fat firm silken tofu (about 4 ounces)	

1. Combine all ingredients in a blender; process until smooth. YIELD: 2 servings (serving size: 1¼ cups).

CALORIES 200; FAT 1.3g (sat 0.6g, mono 0.1g, poly 0.3g); PROTEIN 9.4g; CARB 38.2g; FIBER 2.3g; CHOL 6mg; IRON 1.6mg; SODIUM 134mg; CALC 231mg

RECIPE BENEFITS: low-fat; low-sodium

Mango Lassi

Watermelon Margaritas

Watermelon Margaritas

A long, tall version of the great summer sipper with only 105 calories.

2 teaspoons sugar
1 lime wedge
3½ cups cubed seeded watermelon
½ cup tequila
2 tablespoons sugar

3 tablespoons fresh lime juice
1 tablespoon Triple Sec (orange-flavored liqueur)
Lime wedges or watermelon balls (optional)

1. Place 2 teaspoons sugar in a saucer. Rub rims of 6 glasses with 1 lime wedge; spin rim of each glass in sugar to coat. Set aside prepared glasses.
2. Combine watermelon and next 4 ingredients in a blender; process until smooth. Fill each prepared glass with ½ cup crushed ice. Add ½ cup margarita to each glass. Garnish with lime wedges or melon balls, if desired. YIELD: 6 servings.

CALORIES 105; FAT 0.2g (sat 0g, mono 0g, poly 0.1g); PROTEIN 0.6g; CARB 14.1g; FIBER 0.4g; CHOL 0mg; IRON 0.2mg; SODIUM 1mg; CALC 7mg

RECIPE BENEFITS: fat-free; low-sodium

Lemon Verbena Gimlet Cocktails

157 calories

If you make this ahead, stir in club soda just before serving.

1 cup water
¼ cup sugar
¼ cup torn verbena leaves
¾ cup dry gin

¾ cup club soda, chilled
¼ cup fresh lime juice (about 2 limes)
Lemon verbena sprigs (optional)
Lime slices (optional)

1. Combine 1 cup water and sugar in a small saucepan. Rub torn verbena to bruise; add to pan. Bring sugar mixture to a boil, stirring gently as needed to dissolve sugar evenly; cook 30 seconds. Remove from heat; cool completely. Strain mixture through a sieve over a bowl; discard solids.
2. Combine sugar mixture, gin, soda, and juice. Serve over ice. Garnish with verbena sprigs and lime slices, if desired. YIELD: 4 servings (serving size: about ½ cup).

CALORIES 157; FAT 0g (sat 0g, mono 0g, poly 0g); PROTEIN 0.1g; CARB 13.9g; FIBER 0.1g; CHOL 0mg; IRON 0mg; SODIUM 10mg; CALC 5mg

RECIPE BENEFITS: fat-free; low-sodium

Rosemary-Peach Cocktails

Rosemary-Peach Cocktails

A heady punch of woodsy rosemary creates an herbaceous riff on the classic Bellini.

¾ **cup water**	2 **ripe peeled peaches, cut into 1-inch pieces**
½ **cup sugar**	1 **(750-milliliter) bottle Champagne or**
1 **(3-inch) rosemary sprig**	**sparkling wine, chilled**

1. Combine first 3 ingredients in a small saucepan; bring to a boil. Remove from heat; cool to room temperature. Strain rosemary syrup through a sieve over a bowl; discard solids. Cover and chill at least 1 hour.
2. Place rosemary syrup and peaches in a blender, and process until smooth. Strain mixture through a sieve over a bowl; cover and chill at least 4 hours. Spoon about 2 tablespoons peach syrup into each of 8 Champagne flutes, and top each serving with about ⅓ cup Champagne. **YIELD:** 8 servings.

CALORIES 126; FAT 0.1g (sat 0g, mono 0.1g, poly 0g); PROTEIN 0.2g; CARB 16.5g; FIBER 0.1g; CHOL 0mg; IRON 0.1mg; SODIUM 1mg; CALC 3mg

RECIPE BENEFITS: low-fat; low-sodium

Sparkling Pomegranate Cocktails

The fruit's polyphenols, a class of antioxidants, likely help your heart. They contribute to the vibrant flavor, too.

1½ **cups pomegranate juice**	6 **lime slices (optional)**
¼ **cup grenadine**	**Pomegranate seeds (optional)**
1 **(750-milliliter) bottle Prosecco or dry**	
sparkling wine, chilled	

1. Combine pomegranate juice and ¼ cup grenadine in a 2-cup glass measure. Divide juice mixture evenly among 6 Champagne flutes or wineglasses. Top each serving evenly with wine, and garnish each serving with lime slices and pomegranate seeds, if desired. **YIELD:** 6 servings (serving size: ¾ cup).

CALORIES 164; FAT 0g (sat 0g, mono 0g, poly 0g); PROTEIN 0.3g; CARB 21g; FIBER 0.3g; CHOL 0mg; IRON 0.1mg; SODIUM 11mg; CALC 11mg

RECIPE BENEFITS: fat-free; low-sodium

Chocolate Cappuccino

The drinks at the local coffee shop can be loaded with calories. This homemade version is not, and you can prepare it in about 5 minutes.

146 calories

1 cup chocolate liqueur	1½ cups scalded whole milk
2 tablespoons maple syrup	¼ teaspoon ground cinnamon
2 cups hot brewed espresso	Chocolate shavings (optional)

1. Combine liqueur and syrup in a microwave-safe dish; heat on HIGH for 30 seconds. Divide liqueur mixture evenly among 8 mugs; add ¼ cup espresso to each. Froth milk; pour about ¼ cup milk into each mug. Top with ground cinnamon; garnish with chocolate shavings, if desired. YIELD: 8 servings.

CALORIES 146; FAT 1.7g (sat 0.9g, mono 0.4g, poly 0.2g); PROTEIN 1.5g; CARB 18.9g; FIBER 0g; CHOL 5mg; IRON 0.2mg; SODIUM 29mg; CALC 57mg

RECIPE BENEFITS: low-fat; low-sodium

Chai

Use this basic chai recipe as a starting point, then alter it to suit your preferences. You might add black peppercorns, vanilla bean seeds, star anise, bay leaves, or allspice, for instance.

200 calories

1½ cups water	1 cinnamon stick, broken
7 cardamom pods, crushed	1 cup whole milk
6 whole cloves	1 tablespoon black tea leaves (such as
4 white peppercorns	Darjeeling or Assam)
1 (½-inch) piece peeled fresh ginger, coarsely chopped	¼ cup honey

1. Combine first 6 ingredients in a medium saucepan; bring to a boil. Cover, reduce heat, and simmer 15 minutes. Add milk and tea; simmer 4 minutes (do not boil). Strain through a fine sieve into a small bowl; discard solids. Add honey to tea mixture, stirring until well blended. YIELD: 2 servings (serving size: about 1 cup).

CALORIES 200; FAT 4g (sat 2.3g, mono 1g, poly 0.2g); PROTEIN 4.1g; CARB 40.4g; FIBER 0.1g; CHOL 12mg; IRON 0.2mg; SODIUM 58mg; CALC 129mg

RECIPE BENEFIT: low-sodium

Chocolate Cappuccino

200-CALORIE RECIPES

Entrées

200
calories

Blackened Catfish

A combination of a few pantry spices lends authentic Cajun flavor to catfish. Sautéed Corn and Cherry Tomatoes is delicious served alone as a side dish or as a relish spooned over the catfish.

1 **tablespoon fresh thyme leaves, minced**
1 **teaspoon onion powder**
1 **teaspoon garlic powder**
1 **teaspoon paprika**
1 **teaspoon black pepper**

½ **teaspoon ground red pepper**
¼ **teaspoon salt**
3 **teaspoons olive oil, divided**
4 **(6-ounce) catfish fillets**

1. Combine first 7 ingredients in a small bowl.

2. Heat a large nonstick skillet over medium-high heat. Add 2 teaspoons oil to pan. Brush fillets with remaining teaspoon olive oil. Rub fillets with spice mixture, and add to pan; cook 3 minutes on each side or until fillets reach desired degree of doneness. YIELD: 4 servings (serving size: 1 fillet).

CALORIES 200; FAT 8.3g (sat 1.7g, mono 3.9g, poly 1.9g); PROTEIN 28.2g; CARB 1.9g; FIBER 0.5g; CHOL 99mg; IRON 0.9mg; SODIUM 220mg; CALC 37mg

RECIPE BENEFITS: low-carb; low-sodium

MENU • *serves 4*

Blackened Catfish

Sautéed Corn and Cherry Tomatoes
Heat 2 teaspoons olive oil in a large nonstick skillet over medium heat. Add 1 minced garlic clove to plan; sauté 1 minute. Add 2 cups fresh corn kernels and 1 cup cherry tomatoes; cook 3 minutes or until vegetables are tender, stirring often. Remove from heat; stir in 3 tablespoons chopped green onions, 1 tablespoon sherry vinegar, 2 teaspoons minced fresh thyme, ½ teaspoon freshly ground black pepper, and ¼ teaspoon salt.

Sunflower Seed–Crusted Orange Roughy

When breading the fish, use one hand for the dry mixture and the other hand for the wet so the panko crumbs don't stick to your hand. Serve with steamed asparagus tossed with grated lemon rind.

200 calories

- 2 large egg whites
- ½ teaspoon freshly ground black pepper
- ½ teaspoon grated lemon rind
- ½ cup Italian-seasoned panko (Japanese breadcrumbs)
- 3 tablespoons unsalted sunflower seed kernels
- 4 (6-ounce) orange roughy fillets (about ½ inch thick)
- Cooking spray
- Lemon slices (optional)

1. Preheat oven to 475°. Place a jelly-roll pan in oven while preheating.

2. Combine first 3 ingredients in a medium bowl; stir with a whisk until foamy. Combine panko and sunflower seed kernels in a shallow dish. Dip fillets in egg white mixture; dredge in panko mixture. Place fillets on a wire rack; let stand 10 minutes.

3. Remove jelly-roll pan from oven; coat pan with cooking spray. Coat fillets with cooking spray; place on pan. Bake at 475° for 10 minutes or until fillets reach desired degree of doneness. Serve with lemon slices, if desired. YIELD: 4 servings (serving size: 1 fillet).

CALORIES 200; FAT 4g (sat 0.3g, mono 1g, poly 2.2g); PROTEIN 31.5g; CARB 9.1g; FIBER 1.7g; CHOL 102mg; IRON 2.4mg; SODIUM 212mg; CALC 21mg

RECIPE BENEFIT: low-fat

CHOICE INGREDIENT: *Asparagus*

When selecting asparagus, reach for green instead of white. The green variety is higher in vitamins A and C and folate. Choose asparagus spears with tight, compact tips and a similar diameter so they'll all cook at the same rate.

Spicy Thai Tuna Cakes with Cucumber Aioli

173 calories

Cool cucumber aioli puts out the fire of the Thai spices in these tuna cakes. Although the cakes are portioned as a main dish, you can also form eight smaller appetizer cakes when entertaining guests.

ENTRÉES

3 (5-ounce) cans Thai chili-flavored tuna (such as Bumble Bee), drained	2 tablespoons chopped fresh cilantro
1 large egg white, lightly beaten	Cooking spray
½ cup panko (Japanese breadcrumbs)	½ cup shredded cucumber
	¼ cup light mayonnaise

1. Combine first 4 ingredients in a medium bowl. Divide tuna mixture into 4 equal portions, shaping each into a ¾-inch-thick patty.

2. Heat a large nonstick skillet over medium heat. Coat pan and patties with cooking spray. Add patties; cook 1 to 2 minutes on each side or until lightly browned.

3. While patties cook, combine cucumber and mayonnaise in a small bowl. Serve with tuna cakes. YIELD: 4 servings (serving size: 1 cake and 2 tablespoons aioli).

CALORIES 173; FAT 9g (sat 1.2g, mono 3.8g, poly 3.6g); PROTEIN 10.1g; CARB 11.9g; FIBER 0.9g; CHOL 26mg; IRON 0.8mg; SODIUM 413mg; CALC 4mg

---

MENU • *serves 4*

Spicy Thai Tuna Cakes with Cucumber Aioli

Orange and Radish Cabbage Slaw
Combine 4 cups shredded napa (Chinese) cabbage, ½ cup sliced radishes, and ⅓ cup orange sections in a large bowl. Combine 2 tablespoons rice vinegar, 1 tablespoon canola oil, 2 teaspoons sugar, and 1 teaspoon dark sesame oil in a small bowl, stirring well with a whisk. Pour vinegar mixture over cabbage mixture; toss gently to coat.

161
calories

Skillet Barbecue Shrimp

This barbecue shrimp recipe can be ready in less than 15 minutes, making it a fast, fabulous ending to a day at the beach or pool. Pair the shrimp with mixed salad greens lightly dressed with extra-virgin olive oil and fresh lemon juice.

¾ cup fat-free Italian dressing (such as Wish-Bone)

2 tablespoons butter

1 tablespoon Worcestershire ground black pepper blend (such as McCormick)

1 teaspoon dried rosemary, crushed

2 pounds large shrimp with tails intact

5 lemon wedges

1. Combine first 4 ingredients in a large skillet; bring to a boil. Add shrimp; cook 6 minutes or until shrimp reach desired degree of doneness, stirring occasionally. Serve with lemon wedges. YIELD: 5 servings (serving size: 5 ounces shrimp and about 1 tablespoon sauce).

CALORIES 161; FAT 6g (sat 3.3g, mono 1.5g, poly 0.7g); PROTEIN 22.1g; CARB 3.8g; FIBER 0.5g; CHOL 214mg; IRON 3.4mg; SODIUM 644mg; CALC 57mg

RECIPE BENEFIT: low-carb

8 Top Secrets of Portion Control

So many invisible factors cause us to eat more than we want. Here are easy tips for becoming "portion aware."

1. Before Eating, Divide the Plate

HERE'S A SIMPLE RULE TO PORTION A PLATE PROPERLY: Divide it in half. Automatically fill one side with fruits or vegetables, leaving the rest for equal parts protein and starch. This way you begin to see what a properly balanced meal looks like. Spaghetti and meatballs? Steak and potatoes? They're only half a meal, incomplete without fruits and vegetables.

2. Pre-Portion Tempting Treats

DON'T SNACK DIRECTLY FROM LARGE PACKAGES. The bigger the package, the more food you'll eat out of it. Head off the mindless munching by pre-measuring decadent treats before indulging to keep your portions in check.

3. Downsize the Dishes

IF YOU'RE ONE OF THE 54 PERCENT OF AMERICANS WHO EAT UNTIL THEIR PLATES ARE CLEAN, make sure those plates are modestly sized. On a standard 8- to 10-inch dinner plate, a portion of spaghetti looks like a meal. On a 12- to 14-inch dinner plate, it looks meager so you're likely to dish out a bigger portion to fill the plate. When researchers gave study participants 34- or 17-ounce bowls and told them to help themselves to ice cream, those with the bigger bowls dished out 31 percent more ice cream.

4. Limit Your Choices

THE MORE OPTIONS YOU HAVE, THE MORE YOU WANT TO TRY. In one study, researchers gave two groups jellybeans to snack on while they watched a movie. One group got six colors, neatly divided into compartments; jellybeans for the other group were jumbled together. Those given a mix ate nearly two times more.

5. Avoid a See-Food Diet

OFFICE WORKERS WHO KEPT CANDY IN CLEAR DISHES ON THEIR DESKS dipped in for a sample 71 percent more often than those who kept their candy out of sight.

6. Turn Off the Television

THE VAST WASTELAND LEADS TO VAST WAISTS. It's not just the couch-sitting. TV distracts you from how much you're eating, and the more you watch, the more you're likely to eat. In a study comparing how much popcorn viewers ate during either a half-hour or an hour show, those who watched more television ate 28 percent more popcorn.

7. Think Before You Drink

POUR CRANBERRY JUICE INTO TWO GLASSES OF EQUAL VOLUME—one short and wide, the other tall and thin. Most people pour 19 percent more cranberry juice in the short glass because the eye is a poor judge of volume in relation to height and width.

8. Serve Good-for-You Foods Family-Style

NOT ALL PORTION-CONTROL STRATEGIES ARE ABOUT EATING LESS. You can have as much as you want of some foods. Place the foods you want your family to eat more of—salads and vegetable sides—within easy reach on the dining table. In a soon-to-be-published study, people who kept baby carrots in plain sight ate 25 percent more of them during a day.

Sautéed Vegetables and Spicy Tofu

Thanks to a seasoned package of tofu, this easy stir-fry comes together in a snap. This dish is delicious served alone, but for heartier fare serve it on top of rice noodles.

1 (16-ounce) package spicy tofu, drained
2 tablespoons olive oil, divided
2 tablespoons fresh lemon juice
½ teaspoon salt
¼ teaspoon crushed red pepper

2 large garlic cloves, pressed
1 large zucchini, halved lengthwise and cut crosswise into thin slices
1 cup thinly sliced red bell pepper
Lemon wedges (optional)

1. Place tofu on several layers of heavy-duty paper towels. Cover tofu with additional paper towels; gently press out moisture. Cut tofu into ½-inch cubes.

2. Combine 1 tablespoon oil and next 4 ingredients in a medium bowl. Set aside.

3. Heat remaining 1 tablespoon oil in a large nonstick skillet over medium-high heat. Add tofu, zucchini, and bell pepper; stir-fry 8 to 10 minutes or until tofu is browned and vegetables are crisp-tender. Add oil mixture; cook 1 minute, stirring gently. Serve with lemon wedges, if desired. YIELD: 4 servings (serving size: 1 cup).

CALORIES 196; FAT 13.7g (sat 2.3g, mono 5g, poly 5g); PROTEIN 15g; CARB 7.9g; FIBER 3.2g; CHOL 0mg; IRON 3mg; SODIUM 302mg; CALC 154mg

INGREDIENT TIP: Reduce meal prep time by using jarred, prepeeled garlic cloves instead of peeling them yourself. Look for them in the refrigerated produce section of your supermarket.

196
calories

178
calories

Mediterranean-Style Frittata

The deep green of the spinach in the frittata and the bright red of the Herb-Crusted Broiled Tomatoes create a vibrant combination for a vitamin-packed brunch. To speed up prep time, prepare the tomatoes while the frittata broils.

2 teaspoons olive oil	⅓ cup (1.3 ounces) crumbled feta cheese with basil and sun-dried tomatoes
¾ cup packed baby spinach	
2 green onions	2 teaspoons salt-free Greek seasoning (such as Cavender's)
4 large egg whites	
6 large eggs	¼ teaspoon salt

1. Preheat broiler.

2. Heat oil in a 10-inch ovenproof skillet over medium heat. While oil heats, coarsely chop spinach and finely chop onions. Combine egg whites, eggs, cheese, Greek seasoning, and salt in a large bowl; stir well with a whisk. Add spinach and onions, stirring well.

3. Add egg mixture to pan; cook until edges begin to set, about 2 minutes. Gently lift edge of egg mixture, tilting pan to allow uncooked egg mixture to come in contact with pan. Cook 2 minutes or until egg mixture is almost set.

4. Broil 2 to 3 minutes or until center is set. Transfer the frittata to a serving platter immediately; cut into 4 wedges. YIELD: 4 servings (serving size: 1 wedge).

CALORIES 178; FAT 12g (sat 4g, mono 4.5g, poly 2.4g); PROTEIN 15.7g; CARB 2.2g; FIBER 0.6g; CHOL 326mg; IRON 1.7mg; SODIUM 438mg; CALC 86mg

RECIPE BENEFIT: low-carb

MENU • *serves 4*

Mediterranean-Style Frittata

Herb-Crusted Broiled Tomatoes
Preheat broiler. Combine ¼ cup whole-wheat panko (Japanese breadcrumbs), 2 tablespoons grated Parmesan cheese, 1 teaspoon dried Italian seasoning, ½ teaspoon black pepper, and ¼ teaspoon seasoned salt in a small bowl. Stir 1 teaspoon melted unsalted butter into breadcrumb mixture. Place 4 tomato halves on a rimmed baking sheet coated with cooking spray. Sprinkle breadcrumb mixture evenly over tomato halves. Broil 3 to 4 minutes or until topping is golden. Serve immediately.

197
calories

Ginger-Lime Beef Stir-Fry

Peppery ginger adds a lively herbal note to this stir-fry. Serve over cellophane noodles.

- 1 tablespoon sugar
- 1 tablespoon grated peeled fresh ginger
- 2 tablespoons fresh lime juice (about 1 lime)
- 1½ teaspoons lower-sodium soy sauce
- ¼ teaspoon crushed red pepper

- 1 tablespoon canola oil
- 12 ounces boneless sirloin steak, cut into thin strips
- ½ cup diagonally cut green onions (optional)
- 4 lime wedges (optional)

1. Combine first 5 ingredients in a small bowl; stir well with a whisk.

2. Heat canola oil in a large nonstick skillet over medium-high heat. Add steak; cook 4 minutes or until browned, stirring frequently. Remove from heat; drizzle evenly with ginger-lime mixture. Garnish with onions and lime wedges, if desired. YIELD: 3 servings (serving size: ⅔ cup).

CALORIES 197; FAT 9g (sat 2g, mono 4.5g, poly 2g); PROTEIN 22.4g; CARB 5.5g; FIBER 0.1g; CHOL 42mg; IRON 2.8mg; SODIUM 197mg; CALC 16mg

RECIPE BENEFIT: low-sodium

CHOICE INGREDIENT: *Ginger*

Look for fresh ginger in the produce section of your supermarket. Choose the freshest, youngest-looking rhizomes you can find because they are more flavorful and tender and less fibrous than old ones.

Spiced Pork Tenderloin

A marinade of sugar, bourbon, Worcestershire sauce, and ground cinnamon infuses this succulent grilled pork tenderloin. Arrange the sliced pork over a bed of Sweet Pea and Fresh Mint Couscous for a beautiful restaurant-style presentation.

2 tablespoons sugar
2 tablespoons bourbon
2 tablespoons Worcestershire sauce
$\frac{1}{2}$ teaspoon ground cinnamon

1 (1-pound) pork tenderloin, trimmed
$\frac{1}{4}$ teaspoon salt
$\frac{1}{4}$ teaspoon freshly ground black pepper
Cooking spray

1. Prepare grill.

2. Combine first 4 ingredients in a large zip-top plastic bag. Add pork to bag; seal and shake well. Let stand 10 minutes, turning frequently.

3. Remove pork from bag, reserving marinade. Sprinkle pork evenly with salt and pepper. Place pork on a grill rack coated with cooking spray; grill 10 minutes on each side or until a thermometer registers 160° (slightly pink), basting with reserved marinade. Remove from grill; let stand 3 minutes before slicing. YIELD: 4 servings (serving size: 3 ounces pork).

CALORIES 178; FAT 4g (sat 1.3g, mono 1.5g, poly 0.3g); PROTEIN 22.5g; CARB 8.2g; FIBER 0.2g; CHOL 63mg; IRON 1.8mg; SODIUM 274mg; CALC 18mg

RECIPE BENEFIT: low-fat

MENU • *serves 4*

Spiced Pork Tenderloin

Sweet Pea and Fresh Mint Couscous
Combine ¾ cup water, ¼ teaspoon salt, and ⅛ teaspoon ground turmeric in a medium saucepan. Bring to a boil. Remove from heat; stir in ½ cup uncooked whole-wheat couscous. Cover and let stand 5 minutes. Place ½ cup frozen petite peas in a mesh strainer. Rinse under warm water; drain well. Add peas and 2 tablespoons chopped fresh mint to couscous. Toss well with a fork.

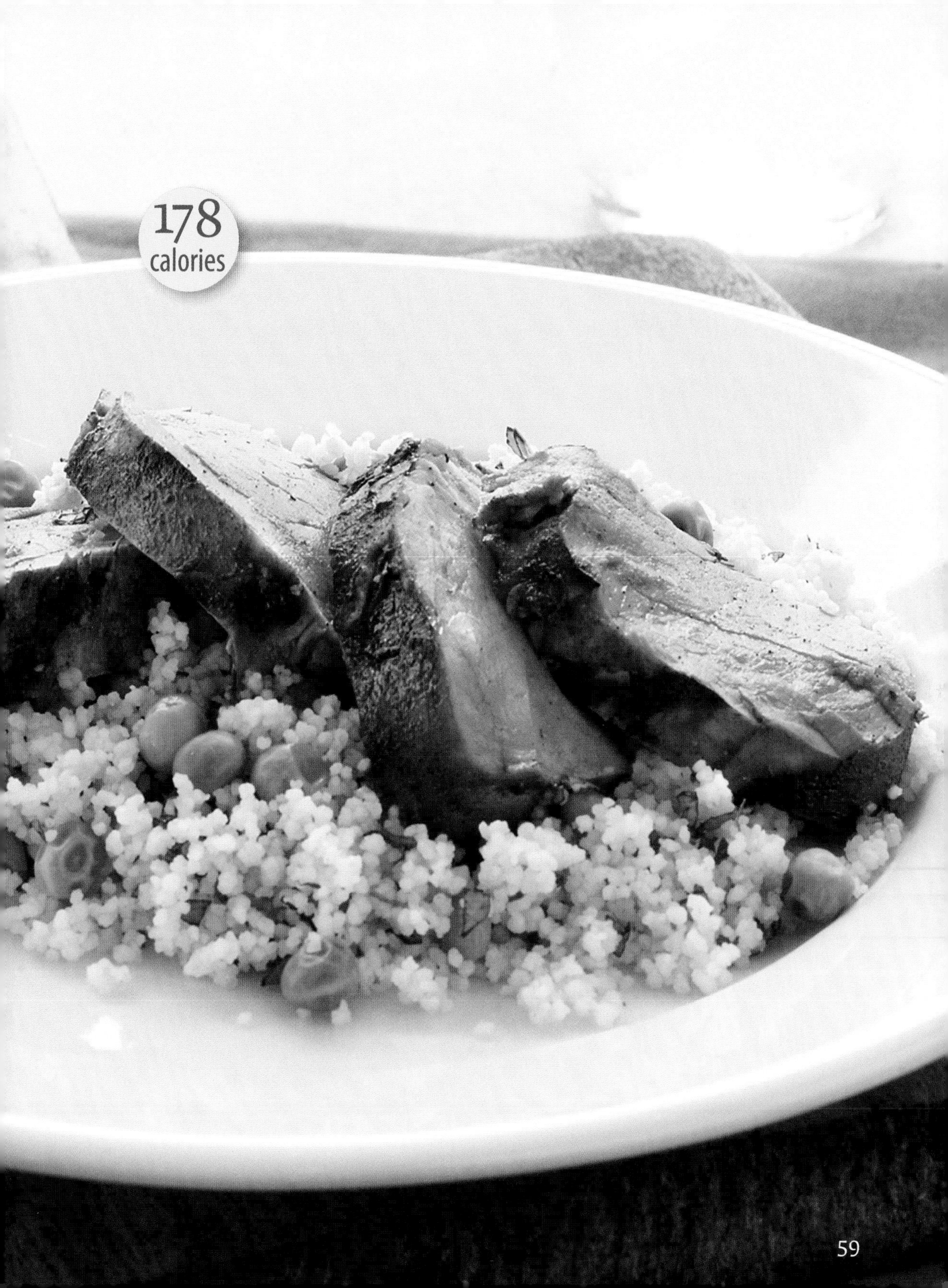
178
calories

Lemon-Caper Pork Medallions

Serve these tender medallions over ½ cup vermicelli tossed with chopped flat-leaf parsley to soak up the savory pan juices, and add steamed green beans.

- 1 (1-pound) pork tenderloin, trimmed
- ½ teaspoon freshly ground black pepper
- ¼ teaspoon salt
- 1 tablespoon olive oil
- ¾ cup fat-free, lower-sodium chicken broth
- 3 tablespoons capers
- 2 tablespoons fresh lemon juice
- 1 lemon, thinly sliced

1. Cut tenderloin crosswise into 8 slices; place between 2 sheets of plastic wrap, and pound to a ¼-inch thickness using a meat mallet or small heavy skillet. Sprinkle pork with pepper and salt. Heat oil in a large nonstick skillet over medium-high heat. Add pork, and cook 2 minutes on each side or until browned.
2. Add broth and remaining ingredients to pan; bring to a boil. Cook 2 to 3 minutes or until liquid is reduced by half. Transfer pork to a serving platter. Spoon sauce and lemon slices over pork medallions. YIELD: 4 servings (serving size: 3 ounces pork and 2 tablespoons sauce).

CALORIES 168; FAT 6g (sat 1.8g, mono 3.4g, poly 0.5g); PROTEIN 23.3g; CARB 1.3g; FIBER 0.3g; CHOL 63mg; IRON 1.3mg; SODIUM 488mg; CALC 9mg

RECIPE BENEFIT: low-carb

168 calories

Meats & Poultry

The USDA doesn't provide specific recommendations for meats and poultry. Instead, it gives a protein recommendation, which you can fulfill from meats, poultry, seafood, eggs, nuts, seeds, peas, and beans.

While the specific amount of protein you need depends on your age, gender, and level of physical activity, most adults need about 1 to 1½ servings (the equivalent of 5 to 6½ ounces of cooked protein or about 30 to 45 grams of protein) per day. For healthy adults, consuming more protein in a day shouldn't be a health concern.

What is a serving?

1 (6-ounce) chicken breast (raw)=1 serving

1 (4-ounce) beef tenderloin steak (raw)=about ⅔ serving

1 (4-ounce) boneless pork loin chop (raw)=⅔ serving

1 (4-ounce) boneless lamb chop (raw)=about ½ serving

1 (¼-pound) burger patty (raw)=about ⅔ serving

1 (4-ounce) boneless veal chop (raw)=½ serving

Choose the Healthiest Meats & Poultry

Although meats and poultry may contain saturated fat and cholesterol, they can still be part of a healthy diet. Here's how:

CHOOSE LEAN CUTS. There are many choices available in the grocery store when it comes to lean meats and poultry. Select cuts of meat with minimal visible fat such as flank steak, tenderloin, loin, sirloin, chuck shoulder, and arm roasts. For the leanest cut of chicken and turkey, choose skinless breasts (light meat).

Meats high in saturated fat tend to have marbling.

TRIM AWAY EXCESS FAT AND REMOVE THE SKIN. Trimming visible fat and removing the skin on meats and poultry will help lower total fat, saturated fat, and calories. Simply removing the skin from a chicken breast reduces the calories by 42 percent and the fat by 88 percent.

PRACTICE PORTION CONTROL. In general, Americans have no problem meeting their protein requirements. And while excess protein may not be harmful to you if you're in good health, it's the excess saturated fat and calories that often come along with it that can lead to problems. One serving of meat is generally about the size of a deck of cards.

199 calories

Chicken Cutlets with Fontina and Fresh Blueberry Sauce

Buttery fontina cheese and a sweet-savory, jewel-toned blueberry sauce turn modest chicken cutlets into an extraordinary dish that family and friends will love.

1 tablespoon butter, divided	3 tablespoons apple juice
³⁄₄ pound chicken cutlets (about 4 cutlets)	1 tablespoon rice wine vinegar
¹⁄₂ teaspoon salt	¹⁄₂ teaspoon Dijon mustard
¹⁄₄ teaspoon freshly ground black pepper	1 cup fresh blueberries
¹⁄₂ cup (2 ounces) shredded fontina cheese	1¹⁄₂ teaspoons minced fresh thyme

1. Melt 1 teaspoon butter in a large nonstick skillet over medium-high heat. Sprinkle chicken with salt and pepper. Add chicken to pan; cook 3 minutes on each side or until desired degree of doneness. Remove chicken to a platter; sprinkle with cheese. Keep warm.

2. Combine apple juice, vinegar, and mustard in a small bowl; stir well with a whisk. Add apple juice mixture to pan; simmer 1 minute. Add blueberries and thyme; simmer 2 minutes. Stir in remaining 2 teaspoons butter. Spoon blueberry sauce over chicken. YIELD: 4 servings (serving size: about 1 chicken cutlet and 2 tablespoons sauce).

CALORIES 199; FAT 8.2g (sat 4.7g, mono 2.2g, poly 0.6g); PROTEIN 23.4g; CARB 7.2g; FIBER 1g; CHOL 73mg; IRON 0.8mg; SODIUM 491mg; CALC 89mg

---

MENU • *serves 4*

Chicken Cutlets with Fontina and Fresh Blueberry Sauce

Ginger-Roasted Green Beans
Preheat oven to 450°. Combine 1 (12-ounce) package pretrimmed green beans, 2 teaspoons olive oil, 2 teaspoons grated peeled fresh ginger, and ¹⁄₈ teaspoon salt on a baking sheet; toss well. Spread beans in a single layer. Bake at 450° for 10 minutes or until crisp-tender.

Balsamic Chicken and Mushrooms

150 calories

Adding water to the mushrooms while they cook makes them tender and saucy.

1 **slice bacon, finely chopped**	1 **(8-ounce) package presliced baby**
¾ **pound chicken cutlets (about 4 cutlets)**	**portobello mushrooms**
3 **tablespoons balsamic vinegar, divided**	½ **cup sliced green onions**
¼ **teaspoon salt, divided**	1 **tablespoon chopped fresh rosemary**
¼ **teaspoon freshly ground black pepper,**	1 **tablespoon water**
divided	**Rosemary sprigs (optional)**

1. Heat a large nonstick skillet over medium-high heat. Add bacon to pan; cook 3 minutes or until crisp. Remove bacon from pan, and drain bacon on paper towel; set aside. Reserve drippings in pan.

2. Brush chicken with 1 tablespoon vinegar and sprinkle with ⅛ teaspoon salt and ⅛ teaspoon pepper. Add chicken to drippings in pan, and cook 3 minutes on each side or until desired degree of doneness. Remove chicken from pan; keep warm.

3. Add mushrooms, green onions, and rosemary to pan. Cook, stirring frequently, 1 minute. Stir in water, remaining 2 tablespoons vinegar, remaining ⅛ teaspoon salt, and remaining ⅛ teaspoon pepper. Cook 6 minutes or until mushrooms are tender, stirring occasionally. Stir in bacon. Spoon mushroom mixture over chicken. Garnish with rosemary springs, if desired. YIELD: 4 servings (serving size: about 1 chicken cutlet and about ⅓ cup mushroom mixture).

CALORIES 150; FAT 4.1g (sat 1.4g, mono 1.6g, poly 0.7g); PROTEIN 22.3g; CARB 5g; FIBER 1g; CHOL 53mg; IRON 1.2mg; SODIUM 248mg; CALC 26mg

RECIPE BENEFITS: low-carb; low-fat

Balsamic Chicken and Mushrooms

Roasted Zucchini

Preheat oven to 475°. Cut 4 medium zucchini in half crosswise; cut each half lengthwise into 4 slices. Toss zucchini with 2 teaspoons olive oil on a baking sheet. Bake at 475° for 13 minutes or until crisp-tender. Sprinkle zucchini with 1 tablespoon chopped fresh oregano, ¼ teaspoon salt, ¼ teaspoon freshly ground black pepper, and ¹⁄₁₆ teaspoon sugar; toss gently to coat.

Vanilla Balsamic Chicken

After scraping the seeds for the sauce, add the vanilla bean pod to a canister of sugar. The scent of the bean will permeate the sugar. Serve the chicken with a tossed green salad.

½ cup fat-free, lower-sodium chicken broth
½ cup balsamic vinegar
¼ cup finely chopped shallots
¼ cup packed brown sugar
¼ teaspoon grated orange rind
¼ cup fresh orange juice
1 (2-inch) piece vanilla bean, split lengthwise
¾ teaspoon salt, divided
16 skinless, boneless chicken thighs (about 2 pounds)
Cooking spray
½ teaspoon freshly ground black pepper
Orange rind strips (optional)

1. Preheat oven to 450°.

2. Combine first 6 ingredients in a small saucepan. Scrape seeds from vanilla bean; stir seeds into broth mixture, reserving the bean for another use. Bring to a boil. Reduce heat, and simmer until reduced to ½ cup (about 20 minutes). Stir in ¼ teaspoon salt.

3. Arrange chicken in a single layer in the bottom of a roasting pan coated with cooking spray. Sprinkle chicken evenly with remaining ½ teaspoon salt and pepper. Bake at 450° for 10 minutes.

4. Brush half of broth mixture over chicken; bake 5 minutes. Brush remaining broth mixture over chicken; bake 15 minutes or until a thermometer registers 180°. Garnish with orange rind, if desired. YIELD: 8 servings (serving size: 2 thighs).

CALORIES 209; FAT 5.5g (sat 1.4g, mono 1.7g, poly 1.4g); PROTEIN 27.5g; CARB 10.9g; FIBER 0.2g; CHOL 115mg; IRON 1.8mg; SODIUM 371mg; CALC 29mg

209
calories

200-CALORIE RECIPES
Salads

QUICK&EASY

Mediterranean Tuna Salad

This Mediterranean-style salad spotlights albacore tuna—a fish that is rich in omega-3 fatty acids. Serve the salad over sliced summer tomatoes with Greek-Style Pita Chips, or stuff the salad in a pita with shredded lettuce for lunch on the go.

1   (12-ounce) can albacore tuna in water, drained and flaked into large chunks
½   cup thinly sliced red onion
2   celery stalks, thinly sliced
2   tablespoons coarsely chopped pitted kalamata olives

2½ tablespoons fresh lemon juice
1   tablespoon olive oil
¼   teaspoon freshly ground black pepper
⅛   teaspoon kosher salt
2   large tomatoes, sliced

1. Combine first 4 ingredients in a medium bowl. Add lemon juice and next 3 ingredients; toss gently to combine. Serve salad over sliced tomatoes.
YIELD: 3 servings (serving size: 1 cup tuna salad and 2 tomato slices).

CALORIES 200; FAT 8g (sat 1g, mono 4.6g, poly 2g); PROTEIN 24.9g; CARB 9.1g; FIBER 2.3g; CHOL 39mg; IRON 0.5mg; SODIUM 593mg; CALC 31mg

---

MENU • *serves 3*

Mediterranean Tuna Salad

Greek-Style Pita Chips
Preheat oven to 400°. Cut 2 (6-inch) pitas into 8 wedges. Separate each wedge into 2 triangles. Place triangles in a single layer on a large baking sheet. Coat top sides of triangles with olive oil–flavored cooking spray; sprinkle evenly with ½ teaspoon dried Greek seasoning. Bake at 400° for 7 to 8 minutes or until crisp and lightly browned; cool.

200
calories

198
calories

Taco Salad with Cilantro-Lime Vinaigrette

An ice-cold beer is all you need to complete the meal with this main-dish salad that's topped with a zesty cilantro-lime dressing. The mushrooms add meaty texture and flavor. Try rolling up the salad mixture in iceberg lettuce leaves for a quick-and-easy variation.

Cooking spray

1 (8-ounce) package presliced mushrooms

2 cups refrigerated meatless fat-free crumbles (such as Lightlife Smart Ground)

2 teaspoons 40%-less-sodium taco seasoning

2 tablespoons finely chopped fresh cilantro

3 tablespoons red wine vinegar

2 tablespoons olive oil

1 teaspoon grated lime rind

1 teaspoon fresh minced garlic

1 (8-ounce) package shredded iceberg lettuce

1 cup ($\frac{1}{8}$-inch-thick) slices red onion

Fresh salsa (optional)

Preshredded reduced-fat Mexican blend cheese (optional)

16 light restaurant-style tortilla chips (such as Tostitos)

1. Heat a large nonstick skillet over medium-high heat; coat pan with cooking spray. Add mushrooms; sauté 3 minutes or until lightly browned. Add crumbles and taco seasoning. Cook 2 minutes or until thoroughly heated; set aside.

2. Combine cilantro and next 4 ingredients in a small bowl, stirring with a whisk; set aside.

3. Layer lettuce, onion, and crumbles mixture evenly on each of 4 plates. Top with salsa, if desired; drizzle evenly with cilantro mixture. Top with cheese, if desired. Serve each salad with tortilla chips. YIELD: 4 servings (serving size: 1½ cups taco salad, about 1 tablespoon dressing, and 4 chips).

CALORIES 198; FAT 11g (sat 1.5g, mono 5.8g, poly 2.5g); PROTEIN 11.7g; CARB 16.7g; FIBER 4.3g; CHOL 0mg; IRON 2.3mg; SODIUM 328mg; CALC 35mg

How to make delicious, showstopping salads.

With a few fresh ingredients, this cool dish is simple to prepare.

Salad Tips

1. BUY FRESH. A salad depends on the quality of its components, especially when it features raw ingredients. Fresh, in-season produce will yield a great-tasting salad.

2. WASH ALL FRUITS, VEGETABLES, AND GREENS THOROUGHLY before using them.

3. CONTRAST CRUNCHY INGREDIENTS WITH CREAMY DRESSINGS; vibrant colors with muted hues; and mellow flavors with spicy, bold ones. The best salads have a balance of textures, colors, and flavors.

4. GO LIGHT. Heavy dressings weigh down ingredients; lighter dressings let other flavors shine through.

5. CHILL YOUR SALAD PLATES AND SERVING BOWL to keep salad greens crisp longer.

6. TO MAKE AHEAD, choose a salad that's meant to be chilled, such as a gelatin salad, a potato salad, a bean salad, or a coleslaw. Green salads should not be assembled until just before serving, or they'll get soggy. You can chop raw vegetables for salads and store them separately in heavy-duty zip-top bags in the refrigerator for up to two days. Toss the vegetables with the greens and add the dressing just before serving.

7. YOU CAN ALSO MAKE SALAD DRESSINGS AHEAD and chill them for several days. Just whisk the dressing before serving. Give an oil-and-vinegar dressing time to return to room temperature before adding it to a salad.

About Greens

BUYING: We prefer to use fresh heads rather than bagged greens because the heads seem to stay crisp longer. Choose greens with fresh-looking, brightly colored leaves with no sign of wilting. Avoid any that are spotted, limp, or yellowing. A brown core does not necessarily indicate poor quality. After lettuce is cut at harvest, the core naturally browns as the cut surface seals to hold in nutrients. If buying bagged salad greens, check the expiration date and choose the freshest.

CLEANING: Wash all greens with cold water. Leafy greens like spinach can harbor sand and other debris; to clean, dunk them in a large bowl, pot, or clean sink filled with cold water. The dirt will sink to the bottom while the greens float to the top. Remove the greens by hand, pour out the water, and repeat the procedure until the water is free of debris. Drain greens on paper towels or with a salad spinner.

STORING: Store washed greens in your refrigerator crisper drawer in zip-top bags with a paper towel to absorb moisture; squeeze out air before sealing. Use within a day or two (use firm lettuces, such as iceberg, within a week).

MEASURING: When measuring greens, don't pack the leaves too tightly in the measuring cup. Instead, place them in the cup, and lightly pat down.

Yucatecan Rice Salad

Yucatecan cuisine combines Spanish, Mexican, and Caribbean flavors. In this spicy recipe, an authentic combination of turmeric, black beans, and olives accompanies the rice. Serve with lemon wedges, if desired.

½ cup water
⅛ teaspoon ground turmeric
½ cup instant whole-grain brown rice (such as Minute)
1 (15-ounce) can black beans, rinsed and drained
½ cup jalapeño-stuffed green olives, coarsely chopped (about 11 olives)

⅓ cup prechopped red onion
3 (0.5-ounce) slices reduced-fat Monterey Jack cheese with jalapeño peppers, cut into ½-inch squares
¼ cup chopped fresh cilantro
1 tablespoon extra-virgin olive oil
Lemon wedges (optional)

1. Bring water and turmeric to a boil in a medium saucepan. Stir in rice; cover, reduce heat, and simmer 5 minutes. Remove from heat. Place rice in a wire mesh strainer; rinse rice with cold water, and drain well.

2. While rice cooks, combine beans and next 5 ingredients in a medium bowl. Add the cooled rice; toss gently until blended. Serve with lemon wedges, if desired.

YIELD: 4 servings (serving size: ¾ cup).

CALORIES 164; FAT 8.3g (sat 1.8g, mono 4.9g, poly 1.3g); PROTEIN 6.4g; CARB 20.9g; FIBER 4.1g; CHOL 8mg; IRON 1.2mg; SODIUM 430mg; CALC 102mg

164
calories

SALADS

Steak Salad with Creamy Horseradish Dressing

Have a steak house–style dinner at home with this tangy, horseradish-seasoned salad boasting melt-in-your-mouth beef tenderloin slices, juicy ruby-red cherry tomatoes, and crunchy cucumber. Pair it with warm breadsticks.

2 (6-ounce) beef tenderloin steaks, trimmed (about ¾ to 1 inch thick)
¼ teaspoon salt
¼ teaspoon freshly ground black pepper
Cooking spray
¾ cup reduced-fat sour cream
¼ cup chopped red onion
2 teaspoons chopped fresh chives
2½ teaspoons prepared horseradish
½ teaspoon fresh lemon juice
¼ teaspoon freshly ground black pepper
1 (6.5-ounce) package sweet butter lettuce blend
1 cup cherry tomatoes, halved
½ cup thinly sliced English cucumber

1. Prepare grill.

2. Sprinkle steaks evenly with salt and pepper. Place steaks on grill rack coated with cooking spray; grill 5 minutes on each side or until desired degree of doneness. Let stand 10 minutes before slicing.

3. While steak stands, combine sour cream and next 5 ingredients in a small bowl. Stir until well blended; chill, if desired.

4. Combine lettuce, tomato, and cucumber in a large bowl; divide evenly among 4 plates. Top salads evenly with steak slices. Drizzle evenly with sour cream mixture. YIELD: 4 servings (serving size: 2 cups salad, about 2 ounces steak, and about 3 tablespoons dressing).

CALORIES 200; FAT 10g (sat 5.4g, mono 2.9g, poly 1.2g); PROTEIN 19.6g; CARB 7.9g; FIBER 1.5g; CHOL 68mg; IRON 1.3mg; SODIUM 79mg; CALC 96mg

RECIPE BENEFIT: low-sodium

Spinach Salad with Grilled Pork Tenderloin and Nectarines

169 calories

Grilling heightens the sweetness and flavor of the nectarines. Because they have such thin skins, nectarines don't require peeling for this dish. However, you can substitute fresh peeled peaches, if you prefer.

1 (1-pound) peppercorn-flavored pork tenderloin, trimmed

3 nectarines, halved

Cooking spray

2 (6-ounce) packages fresh baby spinach

¼ cup light balsamic vinaigrette

¼ cup (1 ounce) crumbled feta cheese

Freshly ground black pepper (optional)

1. Prepare grill.

2. Cut pork horizontally through center of meat, cutting to, but not through, other side using a sharp knife; open flat as you would a book. Place pork and nectarine halves, cut sides down, on grill rack coated with cooking spray. Grill pork 5 minutes on each side or until a thermometer registers 160°. Grill nectarine halves 4 to 5 minutes on each side or until thoroughly heated. Remove pork and nectarine halves from grill. Let pork rest 10 minutes.

3. Cut nectarine halves into slices. Thinly slice pork. Combine spinach and vinaigrette in a large bowl; toss gently to coat.

4. Divide spinach mixture evenly among 6 plates. Top each serving evenly with nectarine slices and pork slices. Sprinkle evenly with cheese and, if desired, pepper. YIELD: 6 servings (serving size: 1⅓ cups spinach salad, ½ nectarine, about 2 ounces pork, and 2 teaspoons cheese).

CALORIES 169; FAT 6g (sat 2g, mono 1.8g, poly 1.3g); PROTEIN 16g; CARB 15.8g; FIBER 3.9g; CHOL 41mg; IRON 2.9mg; SODIUM 766mg; CALC 86mg

SALADS

CHOICE INGREDIENT: *Nectarines*

Think of nectarines and peaches as fraternal twins. Nectarines have a smooth skin, while peaches are covered with soft fuzz. Otherwise, the two fruits are indistinguishable and can be used interchangeably in recipes. The meat of clingstone nectarines and peaches adheres to the pits; these varieties are available early in the season. Freestone varieties—in which the pit easily pulls away from the fruit—begin to ripen mid-season (late June to early July).

Essential Salad Greens

Every salad starts with a base, and—more often than not—that's a bed of fresh greens.

SALADS

ARUGULA: This peppery green's assertive flavor is widely used in Italian cuisine. It's slightly bitter and has a hint of mustard. The prime season for arugula is spring, when its leaves are tender and less bitter. Spinach makes a milder substitute.

BUTTER LETTUCE: Named for its buttery-textured leaves, this lettuce has a slightly sweet flavor. Handle the leaves gently; they bruise easily. Varieties include Boston lettuce and the slightly smaller Bibb lettuce.

ICEBERG LETTUCE: This cool, crunchy head lettuce can hold its texture for hours in a heavy dressing, so it's ideal for make-ahead layered salads. When stored properly, it can keep in the refrigerator for up to a week—much longer than its high-end cousins.

LEAF LETTUCE (GREEN, RED, AND OAK LEAF): This variety has leaves that splay from a central root. The most common are green leaf; red leaf, with its distinctive burgundy tinge; and oak leaf, which is so named because its shape is similar to an oak leaf. Leaf lettuce tends to be more perishable than head lettuce.

MESCLUN: Often packaged as gourmet salad greens, this is a mixture of tender, young salad greens, such as arugula, dandelion, frisée, oak leaf, radicchio, and sorrel. In large supermarkets, mesclun is sold loose in plastic-lined baskets or boxes. Customers bag and weigh the amount of greens they need.

RADICCHIO: Also known as Italian chicory, this bitter pepper-flavored plant has stark white veins and dramatic coloring that ranges from magenta to maroon. Depending on the variety, it can grow in a small rounded head or have narrow leaves that taper.

ROMAINE: Romaine leaves grow in heads and range in color from dark green outer leaves to a yellowish-green heart in the center. The lettuce of choice for Caesar salads, romaine adds crisp texture to any lettuce mix.

SPINACH: Choose spinach leaves that are crisp and dark green with a fresh fragrance. We like baby spinach because its mild, tender leaves are prime for enjoying raw in salads, and there's no need to trim the stems.

WATERCRESS: This member of the mustard family has small, crisp dark green leaves with a sharp, peppery flavor. Pungent-flavored arugula makes a good substitute. If you don't care for the sharp flavor, you can use spinach.

Heirloom Tomato and Goat Cheese Salad with Bacon Dressing

Three harmonious flavors converge in this simple salad: smoky bacon, earthy goat cheese, and acidic tomatoes. Serve with a warm baguette slice and a glass of dry white wine to complete the meal.

2	heirloom tomatoes, sliced
1	(4-ounce) package goat cheese, sliced
½	cup vertically sliced onion
2	cups bagged baby spinach leaves
6	center-cut 30%-less fat bacon slices
¼	cup cider vinegar
2	tablespoons honey
¼	teaspoon kosher salt
½	teaspoon freshly ground black pepper
¼	cup minced green onions (1 large)

1. Arrange layers of tomato slices and next 3 ingredients evenly on each of 4 serving plates.

2. Cook bacon in a skillet over medium heat until crisp. Remove bacon from pan, reserving 1 tablespoon drippings in pan; drain bacon.

3. Add vinegar and next 4 ingredients to drippings in pan, stirring with a whisk. Remove pan from heat. Crumble bacon, and add to pan, stirring with a whisk.

4. Drizzle salads evenly with dressing. YIELD: 4 servings (serving size: 1 salad and 2 tablespoons dressing).

CALORIES 173; FAT 8.5g (sat 4.9g, mono 2.4g, poly 1.2g); PROTEIN 10.2g; CARB 14.4g; FIBER 1.5g; CHOL 21mg; IRON 1.7mg; SODIUM 457mg; CALC 65mg

CHOICE INGREDIENT: *Heirloom Tomatoes*

We recommend using heirloom tomatoes, which are grown from the seeds of old-fashioned varieties, because of their full-bodied flavor and dazzling palette of colors. They vary from red to yellow and from green to purplish black. Look for them at farmers' markets during the summer months.

173
calories

184
calories

Chicken BLT Salad with Creamy Avocado–Horned Melon Dressing

A creamy dressing featuring horned melon lends subtle cucumber flavor to this crisp, colorful chicken BLT salad. You can store the leftover dressing in the refrigerator for up to three days.

3 cups sliced cooked chicken breast (about 1 pound)	¼ cup low-fat buttermilk
1 tomato, cut into wedges	2 tablespoons fresh lemon juice
1 (10-ounce) package romaine salad	2 tablespoons water
1 horned melon	¼ teaspoon salt
1 small ripe peeled avocado	¼ teaspoon freshly ground black pepper
1 small garlic clove	3 center-cut bacon slices, cooked and crumbled

1. Combine first 3 ingredients in a large bowl; toss well.

2. Cut horned melon in half lengthwise; scoop out pulp. Place pulp in a fine sieve over a bowl. Press pulp with the back of a spoon to extract juice; discard juice. Place pulp and next 7 ingredients in a blender or food processor; process until smooth. Drizzle ¾ cup dressing over salad; reserve remaining ¾ cup dressing for another use. Sprinkle bacon over top of salad. YIELD: 6 servings (serving size: about 1¾ cups salad).

CALORIES 184; FAT 7g (sat 1.8g, mono 3.1g, poly 1.3g); PROTEIN 24.5g; CARB 5.8g; FIBER 2.9g; CHOL 63mg; IRON 1.5mg; SODIUM 186mg; CALC 42mg

RECIPE BENEFIT: low-sodium

CHOICE INGREDIENT: *Horned Melons*

Also known as kiwano melons, horned melons grow in New Zealand and are now commonly found in many grocery stores. They have a yellow-orange spiked exterior and a green jellylike flesh similar in flavor to a cucumber. The fruit has broad applications in savory and sweet dishes. Strain out the seeds, and use the pulp in salad dressings, soups, sauces, and sorbets.

Greek Salad Bowl

Crispy thin breadsticks such as grissini or low-fat crackers make an ideal accompaniment to this flavor-packed Mediterranean salad. If you are watching your sodium intake, check the hearts of palm and artichoke hearts labels carefully; sodium levels vary widely among brands.

- 8 cups torn romaine lettuce
- 2 cups chopped cooked chicken breast (about ¾ pound)
- 1 (14-ounce) can hearts of palm (such as Vigo), drained and sliced
- 1 (14-ounce) can quartered artichoke hearts (such as Vigo), drained
- 1 cup grape tomatoes, halved
- ½ cup pitted kalamata olives, halved
- ½ cup thinly sliced red onion
- ⅓ cup light Greek vinaigrette with oregano and feta cheese (such as Good Seasons)

1. Combine all ingredients in a large bowl; toss well to coat. Serve immediately.

YIELD: 6 servings (serving size: 2 cups).

CALORIES 182; FAT 8g (sat 1.4g, mono 3.7g, poly 2.1g); PROTEIN 18.1g; CARB 11.1g; FIBER 3.2g; CHOL 40mg; IRON 3.4mg; SODIUM 695mg; CALC 67mg

CHOICE INGREDIENT: *Romaine Leaves*

Romaine leaves grow in heads and range in color from dark-green outer leaves to a yellowish-green heart in the center. Baby romaine leaves, which are available prewashed in packages, offer the same pleasing, slightly bitter flavor of regular romaine. But stick with the full-sized version for the signature crunch that comes from a romaine leaf's succulent center vein.

SALADS

182
calories

All About Oils

COOKING OILS ARE INDISPENSABLE. They lubricate food, distribute heat, facilitate browning, create tenderness in baked goods, and provide a smooth, rich mouthfeel. Many also impart their own unique flavors to dishes. Other oils—notably regular olive oil and canola oil—taste more neutral, allowing the flavors of the food to shine.

Light, oxygen, and heat cause oil to spoil rapidly, so store in tightly sealed, colored-glass or opaque containers in a cool, dark place; a cabinet or pantry is ideal.

Anatomy of Oil

• **OILS ARE LIQUID FATS (AS OPPOSED TO SOLID FATS, SUCH AS BUTTER OR SHORTENING)—**so 100 percent of any oil's calories come from fat.

• **OILS ARE DERIVED FROM PLANT SOURCES—** nuts (such as walnuts), seeds (such as sesame seeds), plants (such as rapeseed), and fruits (such as olives or avocados).

• **MANY OILS ARE LOW IN SATURATED FAT** and high in heart-healthy monounsaturated and polyunsaturated fats.

Oils and Nutrition

SEVERAL COMPREHENSIVE STUDIES HAVE REVEALED THAT OVERALL FAT CONSUMPTION ISN'T AS MUCH OF A CONCERN TO OUR HEALTH AS THE TYPES OF FAT WE CONSUME. Substituting mono-unsaturated and polyunsaturated fats (like those found in cooking oils) for saturated and trans fats (found mostly in fatty meats and processed foods, respectively) may actually reduce harmful LDL, and mono-unsaturated fat may raise beneficial HDL cholesterol, which can help lower your risk of heart disease.

Oil Glossary

EXTRA-VIRGIN OLIVE OIL: Extra-virgin olive oil has a rich range of flavors, from pungent and bold to smooth and buttery. Because the flavor of extra-virgin olive oil can diminish with heat, it's often used to finish a dish, drizzled over pasta, or whisked into a vinaigrette (though many chefs cook with it, too).

REGULAR OLIVE OIL: Also called "pure" or "light" olive oil, which are simply marketing tags and not an indication of nutritional qualities, this olive oil is a blend of refined olive oil and extra-virgin olive oil. It costs less and has a mild flavor. Use it when you want to preserve the flavors of the food rather than impart the character of the oil to it. We often use it for sautés or stir-fries.

CANOLA OIL: Derived from a strain of rapeseed in Canada in the 1970s that yields oil with lower acidity than traditional grapeseed, this oil's name is an amalgam of the words "Canada" and "oil." Canola oil continues to be a major export crop for its namesake country. It's high in both polyunsaturated and monounsaturated fats and very low in saturated fat. Its neutral flavor makes it a good choice when you don't want to detract from the flavors of the food.

SESAME OIL: This oil is pressed from crushed sesame seeds. The lighter-colored oil comes from raw seeds and has a mild, neutral taste. Dark sesame oil, also called toasted sesame oil, has been pressed from toasted sesame seeds and has an intense, nutty flavor and aroma. Both are considered a seasoning.

WALNUT OIL: Unrefined walnut oil tastes just like the nut from which it comes. It's rich and flavorful (especially if made from toasted walnuts) and perfect as a finishing drizzle on salads, rice, pasta, or even desserts like tarte tatin or rice pudding.

CHOICE INGREDIENT: *Pomegranate Juice*

Antioxidant-rich pomegranate juice has found a place in a healthful diet that stretches beyond a quick cup of juice with breakfast. Pomegranate juice has a rich and tangy flavor, which makes it an ideal ingredient to use in simple salad dressings and pan sauces with short ingredient lists.

Chicken, Spinach, and Blueberry Salad with Pomegranate Vinaigrette

Sweet blueberries pair well with distinctive blue cheese in this chicken salad, while a bold-flavored vinaigrette lightly coats the tender baby spinach leaves.

Cooking spray

8 chicken breast tenders (about ¾ pound)

1½ teaspoons coarsely ground black pepper

¼ teaspoon salt

½ cup pomegranate juice

3 tablespoons sugar

3 tablespoons balsamic vinegar

1 tablespoon canola oil

1 teaspoon grated orange rind

8 cups bagged baby spinach

½ cup thinly sliced red onion

1 cup fresh blueberries

¼ (1 ounce) cup crumbled blue cheese

1. Heat a grill pan or large nonstick skillet over medium-high heat. Coat pan with cooking spray. Sprinkle chicken with pepper and salt. Coat chicken with cooking spray, and add to pan. Cook 3 to 4 minutes on each side or until done.

2. Combine pomegranate juice and next 4 ingredients in a small bowl. Stir with a whisk until blended.

3. Divide spinach evenly on each of 4 serving plates; drizzle evenly with vinaigrette. Arrange chicken, onion, and blueberries evenly over spinach. Sprinkle evenly with cheese. YIELD: 4 servings (serving size: 2 cups spinach, 2 chicken tenders, 3 tablespoons vinaigrette, 2 tablespoons onion, ¼ cup blueberries, and 1 tablespoon cheese).

CALORIES 200; FAT 4.4g (sat 1.7g, mono 1.6g, poly 0.7g); PROTEIN 23g; CARB 18.5g; FIBER 3.7g; CHOL 56mg; IRON 2.4mg; SODIUM 377mg; CALC 95mg

RECIPE BENEFIT: low-fat

170
calories

SALADS

Chicken Salad with Asparagus and Creamy Dill Dressing

This tasty salad is perfect for evenings when you're looking for a quick, no-fuss meal. We hand-pulled large pieces of chicken from a cooked chicken breast to achieve a chunky texture. Serve with crackers to complete the meal.

2½ cups (2-inch) diagonally cut asparagus
½ cup reduced-fat mayonnaise
½ cup nonfat buttermilk
1 tablespoon chopped fresh dill
1 tablespoon fresh lemon juice
¼ teaspoon kosher salt
¼ teaspoon freshly ground black pepper
2 cups coarsely shredded cooked chicken breast (about 8 ounces)
½ cup thinly sliced radishes
8 tomato slices (about 1 large)
Freshly ground black pepper (optional)

1. Steam asparagus, covered, 3 minutes or until crisp-tender. Drain and plunge asparagus into ice water; drain.

2. Combine mayonnaise and next 5 ingredients in a medium bowl, stirring well with a whisk.

3. Combine asparagus, chicken, radishes, and dressing in a large bowl; toss well. Arrange 2 tomato slices on each of 4 plates; top each serving with 1 cup chicken mixture. Sprinkle with pepper, if desired. YIELD: 4 servings (serving size: 1 salad and 2 tablespoons dressing).

CALORIES 170; FAT 4.3g (sat 0.6g, mono 1.7g, poly 1.5g); PROTEIN 21.2g; CARB 12.2g; FIBER 2.8g; CHOL 49mg; IRON 2.6mg; SODIUM 467mg; CALC 79mg

RECIPE BENEFIT: low-fat

MAKE-AHEAD TIP: Reduced-fat mayonnaise, nonfat buttermilk, fresh dill, and fresh lemon juice form the base for superfast homemade Creamy Dill Dressing. Make extra to keep on hand to drizzle over side salads or serve as a vegetable dip. We recommend using fresh dill, but in a pinch, you can substitute 1 teaspoon of dried dill.

SALADS

Feta-Chicken Couscous Salad with Basil

Serve this salad with crispbreads and red pepper hummus for a light summer meal.

1¼ cups water
⅔ cup uncooked whole wheat couscous
1 cup diced cooked chicken breast (such as Tyson)
¼ cup chopped fresh basil
3 tablespoons capers, rinsed and drained
1 tablespoon extra-virgin olive oil
1 teaspoon grated lemon rind
1 tablespoon fresh lemon juice
2 cups mixed baby salad greens
¼ cup (1 ounce) crumbled reduced-fat feta cheese

1. Bring 1¼ cups water to a boil in a medium saucepan. Add couscous; cover and let stand 5 minutes.

2. While couscous stands, combine chicken and next 5 ingredients in a large bowl, tossing gently to coat.

3. Fluff couscous with a fork. Add couscous, salad greens, and cheese to chicken mixture; toss gently to coat. YIELD: 4 servings (serving size: 1 cup).

CALORIES 200; FAT 7g (sat 1.8g, mono 2.9g, poly 0.8g); PROTEIN 17.2g; CARB 20.7g; FIBER 2.7g; CHOL 33mg; IRON 1.1mg; SODIUM 366mg; CALC 56mg

CHOICE INGREDIENT: *Lemons*

Whether using juice, lemon zest (rind), or slices, the acidity of lemon adds to the final balance of flavor in all types of food, from savory to sweet. Look for lemons with smooth, brightly colored skin that are heavy for their size. Store them up to 3 weeks in the refrigerator. Allow lemons to come to room temperature before juicing to ensure that you get the most juice from each lemon.

Easy Homemade Salad Dressings

Whisk together one of these outstanding dressings to turn any bed of greens into a gourmet salad.

Poppy Seed Dressing

3 tablespoons sugar	1 tablespoon poppy seeds
3 tablespoons light mayonnaise	1 tablespoon white wine vinegar
2 tablespoons fat-free milk	

1. Combine all ingredients in a small bowl, stirring with a whisk. YIELD: about ⅔ cup (serving size: 1 tablespoon).

CALORIES 35; FAT 1.9g (sat 0.3g, mono 0.1g, poly 0.3g); PROTEIN 0.3g; CARB 4.4g; FIBER 0.1g; CHOL 2mg; IRON 0.1mg; SODIUM 38mg; CALC 16mg

Honeyed Lemon-Dijon Vinaigrette

¼ cup chopped fresh dill	4 teaspoons honey
¼ cup white wine vinegar	2 teaspoons Dijon mustard
2 tablespoons chopped red onion	¾ teaspoon freshly ground black pepper
2 tablespoons capers	½ teaspoon hot pepper sauce
1 tablespoon grated lemon rind	2 garlic cloves, minced
2 tablespoons fresh lemon juice	⅓ cup boiling water
1 teaspoon salt	¼ cup extra-virgin olive oil

1. Place first 12 ingredients in a blender; process until smooth. Add water and oil; process until well combined. YIELD: about 1½ cups (serving size: 1 tablespoon).

CALORIES 27; FAT 2.4g (sat 0.3g, mono 1.8g, poly 0.2g); PROTEIN 0.1g; CARB 1.6g; FIBER 0.1g; CHOL 0mg; IRON 0.1mg; SODIUM 133mg; CALC 2mg

Blue Cheese Salad Dressing

1 cup light mayonnaise
2 tablespoons cider vinegar
1 tablespoon canola oil
½ teaspoon dried oregano
¼ teaspoon salt

¼ teaspoon freshly ground black pepper
1 (8-ounce) carton fat-free sour cream
1 garlic clove, crushed
½ cup (2 ounces) crumbled blue cheese

1. Combine first 8 ingredients, stirring with a whisk. Stir in cheese. Cover and refrigerate at least 3 hours. YIELD: 2½ cups (serving size: 1 tablespoon).

CALORIES 34; FAT 2.8g (sat 0.7g, mono 0.3g, poly 0.1g); PROTEIN 0.6g; CARB 1.4g; FIBER 0g; CHOL 4mg; IRON 0mg; SODIUM 94mg; CALC 17mg

Balsamic Vinaigrette

½ cup basil leaves
⅓ cup balsamic or sherry vinegar
⅓ cup finely chopped shallots
¼ cup water

2 tablespoons honey
1 tablespoon olive oil
¼ teaspoon freshly ground black pepper

1. Place all ingredients in a blender; process until smooth. YIELD: 1 cup (serving size: 1 tablespoon).

CALORIES 19; FAT 0.9g (sat 0.1g, mono 0.7g, poly 0.1g); PROTEIN 0.2g; CARB 2.9g; FIBER 0.1g; CHOL 0mg; IRON 0.1mg; SODIUM 1mg; CALC 4mg

Citrus Vinaigrette

3 tablespoons fresh orange juice
1½ tablespoons fresh lime juice
2½ teaspoons extra-virgin olive oil
2 teaspoons honey

1 teaspoon red wine vinegar
¼ teaspoon salt
⅛ teaspoon freshly ground black pepper

1. Combine all ingredients, stirring with a whisk. YIELD: ¼ cup (serving size: 1 tablespoon).

CALORIES 43; FAT 3g (sat 0.4g, mono 2.1g, poly 0.4g); PROTEIN 0.1g; CARB 4.7g; FIBER 0.1g; CHOL 0mg; IRON 0.1mg; SODIUM 148mg; CALC 3mg

200-CALORIE RECIPES

Soups

Thai Coconut Shrimp Soup

Freshly squeezed lime juice is the secret ingredient in this recipe. It balances and brightens the flavors and adds just the right amount of tartness to the soup.

1 pound peeled and deveined large shrimp
1 tablespoon salt-free Thai seasoning (such as Frontier)
Cooking spray
1 cup refrigerated prechopped tricolor bell pepper

2½ cups fat-free, lower-sodium chicken broth
1 tablespoon fish sauce
1 (13.5-ounce) can light coconut milk
1 tablespoon fresh lime juice
Chopped fresh cilantro (optional)

1. Sprinkle shrimp with Thai seasoning; toss well. Heat a large Dutch oven coated with cooking spray over medium-high heat. Coat seasoned shrimp with cooking spray, and add to pan; sauté 2 minutes or until shrimp almost reach desired degree of doneness. Remove shrimp from pan; set aside. Recoat pan with cooking spray; add bell pepper, and sauté 2 minutes.

2. Add chicken broth and fish sauce to bell pepper in pan; bring to a boil. Reduce heat; simmer 5 minutes. Stir in coconut milk and reserved shrimp. Cook 2 minutes or until thoroughly heated. Remove from heat; stir in lime juice. Stir in cilantro, if desired. YIELD: 4 servings (serving size: 1¾ cups).

CALORIES 185; FAT 6g (sat 4.5g, mono 0.2g, poly 0.4g); PROTEIN 21.6g; CARB 12.4g; FIBER 0.6g; CHOL 168mg; IRON 4.3mg; SODIUM 858mg; CALC 38mg

SOUPS

CHOICE INGREDIENT: *Light Coconut Milk*

Coconut milk is a staple ingredient in Asian cuisine that adds rich flavor to soups and curries. Unfortunately, it's high in saturated fat. Light (or "lite") coconut milk has less fat and about a quarter of the calories of regular coconut milk. Look for canned milk in the ethnic-foods section of most supermarkets.

185
calories

105

Oriental Soup with Mushrooms, Bok Choy, and Shrimp

You can use most any greens in place of the baby bok choy, including spinach or napa (Chinese) cabbage.

2 teaspoons dark sesame oil	1 tablespoon lower-sodium soy sauce
Cooking spray	3 cups coarsely chopped baby bok choy
2 (3½-ounce) packages shiitake mushrooms, trimmed and thinly sliced	2 tablespoons sliced green onions
	2 tablespoons chopped fresh cilantro
3 tablespoons chopped peeled fresh ginger	1 pound peeled and deveined shrimp
3 cups fat-free, lower-sodium chicken broth	¼ cup fresh lime juice (about 3 limes)
3 cups water	

1. Heat oil in a large Dutch oven coated with cooking spray over medium-high heat; sauté mushrooms and ginger 5 minutes or until liquid evaporates and mushrooms darken.

2. Add broth, 3 cups water, and soy sauce; bring mixture to a boil. Stir in bok choy and next 3 ingredients; cover, reduce heat, and simmer 3 minutes or until shrimp reach desired degree of doneness. Stir in lime juice just before serving.

YIELD: 6 servings (serving size: 1⅔ cups).

CALORIES 102; FAT 2g (sat 0.4g, mono 0.1g, poly 0.3g); PROTEIN 15.1g; CARB 4.9g; FIBER 0.9g; CHOL 112mg; IRON 2.7mg; SODIUM 534mg; CALC 63mg

RECIPE BENEFITS: low-carb; low-fat

MENU • *serves 6*

Oriental Soup with Mushrooms, Bok Choy, and Shrimp

Sesame Wonton Crisps
Preheat oven to 400°. Combine 2 teaspoons dark sesame oil and 1 teaspoon water in a small bowl; set aside. Place 18 wonton wrappers on a baking sheet coated with cooking spray. Brush evenly with oil mixture. Sprinkle evenly with 1 teaspoon sesame seeds, ¼ teaspoon salt, and ⅛ teaspoon five-spice powder. Bake at 400° for 5 minutes or until browned and crispy.

102
calories

194
calories

New England Clam Chowder

Traditional clam chowder recipes are usually loaded with fat and calories. Here's a version that slims it down but still keeps all the delicious flavor and yummy goodness of the original.

4   (6½-ounce) cans chopped clams, undrained
2   (8-ounce) bottles clam juice
4   bacon slices
1   cup chopped onion
1   cup chopped celery
1   garlic clove, minced
3   cups cubed red potato
1½ teaspoons chopped fresh thyme
¼   teaspoon black pepper
3   parsley sprigs
1   bay leaf
2   cups 2% reduced-fat milk
¼   cup all-purpose flour
½   cup half-and-half
Thyme sprigs (optional)

1. Drain clams through a colander into a bowl, reserving liquid and clams. Combine clam liquid and clam juice.

2. Cook bacon in a Dutch oven over medium-high heat until crisp. Remove bacon from pan, reserving 2 teaspoons drippings in pan. Crumble bacon, and set aside. Add onion, celery, and garlic to pan, and sauté 8 minutes or until tender. Add clam juice mixture, potato, and next 4 ingredients; bring to a boil. Cover, reduce heat, and simmer 15 minutes or until potato is tender.

3. Combine milk and flour, stirring with a whisk until smooth; add to pan. Stir in clams and half-and-half. Cook 5 minutes. Discard bay leaf. Serve with bacon. Garnish with thyme sprigs, if desired. YIELD: 8 servings (serving size: 1¼ cups chowder and 1½ teaspoons bacon).

CALORIES 194; FAT 5.4g (sat 2.7g, mono 1.9g, poly 0.4g); PROTEIN 12.3g; CARB 23.7g; FIBER 1.4g; CHOL 32mg; IRON 2.2mg; SODIUM 639mg; CALC 111mg

Smoky Black Bean Soup with Avocado-Lime Salsa

The rich avocado topping is the secret ingredient in this recipe. It soothes the slow burn from the smoky chipotle heat and adds a burst of fresh flavor.

1 (15-ounce) can black beans, rinsed and drained
1 cup water
1 (14.5-ounce) can fire-roasted diced tomatoes, undrained
½ cup chipotle salsa

1 teaspoon ground cumin
1 cup diced peeled avocado
1 lime
2 tablespoons finely chopped fresh cilantro
⅛ teaspoon salt
Reduced-fat sour cream (optional)

1. Place beans in a medium saucepan; mash beans slightly with a potato masher. Stir in water and next 3 ingredients. Cover and bring to a boil over high heat; reduce heat, and simmer 8 minutes. Uncover and cook 2 minutes or until soup is slightly thickened.

2. While soup cooks, place avocado in a small bowl. Grate rind from lime, and squeeze juice to measure ½ teaspoon and 1 tablespoon, respectively; add to avocado. Add cilantro and salt. Toss gently.

3. Ladle soup evenly into each of 4 bowls; top evenly with avocado mixture, and, if desired, sour cream. YIELD: 4 servings (serving size: 1 cup soup and ¼ cup salsa).

CALORIES 172; FAT 5.7g (sat 0.9g, mono 3.4g, poly 0.8g); PROTEIN 7.4g; CARB 29.7g; FIBER 11g; CHOL 0mg; IRON 3.1mg; SODIUM 572mg; CALC 60mg

RECIPE BENEFIT: high-fiber

KITCHEN TIP: Canned beans are more convenient than dried beans. For the best results, rinse thoroughly with tap water before using, and drain in a colander. Rinsing canned beans gets rid of the thick liquid in the can and reduces the sodium by 40 percent.

172
calories

200
calories

Cheese Tortellini and Vegetable Soup

This hearty soup is reminiscent of the Italian classic minestrone. Though minestrone traditionally uses macaroni, we've substituted fresh cheese tortellini for better flavor and to speed preparation. Serve with a tossed spinach salad to round out the meal.

1   (14½-ounce) can diced tomatoes with garlic and onion, undrained
1   (11½-ounce) can condensed bean with bacon soup (such as Campbell's), undiluted
3   cups water

1   (16-ounce) package frozen Italian-style vegetables
¾   teaspoon dried Italian seasoning
¼   teaspoon freshly ground black pepper
½   (9-ounce) package fresh cheese tortellini
¼   cup grated Parmesan cheese

1. Combine first 6 ingredients in a 4-quart saucepan; cover and bring to a boil over high heat. Add pasta; reduce heat to medium. Cook, partially covered, 7 minutes or until pasta and vegetables are tender. Stir in cheese. YIELD: 6 servings (serving size: 1⅓ cups).

CALORIES 200; FAT 4g (sat 1.4g, mono 0.7g, poly 0.3g); PROTEIN 10.3g; CARB 31.3g; FIBER 5.4g; CHOL 11mg; IRON 2.1mg; SODIUM 920mg; CALC 66mg

RECIPE BENEFITS: low-fat; high-fiber

INGREDIENT TIP: Fresh tortellini is available with a variety of fillings, including cheese, chicken, and mushroom. You can substitute any flavor you like for the cheese tortellini (nutritional information may vary). Look for fresh tortellini in the refrigerated section of your grocery store.

103
calories

French Onion Soup

Traditionally, cheese toast tops a classic bistro-style French onion soup. However, we decided to omit it from this rich soup and add a gourmet grilled sandwich on the side instead. It's the perfect accompaniment.

1 tablespoon vegetable oil
3 sweet onions, cut in half vertically and thinly sliced (about 1¾ pounds)

5 sprigs fresh thyme
2 (14-ounce) cans fat-free, lower-sodium beef broth

1. Heat oil in a large Dutch oven over medium-high heat. Add onion and thyme; cover and cook 20 minutes, stirring occasionally. Stir in broth; simmer 4 minutes. Discard thyme sprigs. YIELD: 4 servings (serving size: 1¼ cups).

CALORIES 103; FAT 3.7g (sat 0.5g, mono 1.2g, poly 1.7g); PROTEIN 3.4g; CARB 15g; FIBER 1.8g; CHOL 0mg; IRON 0.6mg; SODIUM 415mg; CALC 41mg

MENU • *serves 4*

French Onion Soup

Gruyère-Thyme Grilled Cheese Sandwiches
Combine ¾ cup (3 ounces) Gruyère cheese, 1 teaspoon fresh thyme leaves, 2 teaspoons Dijon mustard, and ¼ teaspoon black pepper in a bowl. Spread filling on 4 (¼-inch-thick) slices Italian bread; top with 4 (¼-inch-thick) slices Italian bread. Heat a large nonstick skillet over medium-high heat. Coat tops of sandwiches with butter-flavored cooking spray. Arrange sandwiches, top side down, in pan; coat bottoms of sandwiches with cooking spray. Cook 2 to 3 minutes on each side or until cheese melts and bread is golden brown.

Beefy Corn and Black Bean Chili

193 calories

This dish has the flavor and aroma of chili that has simmered all day—and only you have to know it hasn't. Dress it up with a dollop of sour cream and sliced green onions, and serve it with Cheesy Cheddar Corn Bread.

1 pound ground round
2 teaspoons salt-free chili powder blend (such as The Spice Hunter)
1 (14-ounce) package frozen seasoned corn and black beans (such as Pictsweet)
1 (14-ounce) can fat-free, lower-sodium beef broth

1 (15-ounce) can seasoned tomato sauce for chili (such as Hunt's Family Favorites)
Reduced-fat sour cream (optional)
Sliced green onions (optional)

1. Combine beef and chili powder blend in a large Dutch oven. Cook 6 minutes over medium-high heat or until beef is browned, stirring to crumble. Drain and return to pan.

2. Stir in frozen corn mixture, broth, and tomato sauce; bring to a boil. Cover, reduce heat, and simmer 10 minutes. Uncover and simmer 5 minutes, stirring occasionally.

3. Ladle chili into bowls. Top each serving with sour cream and onions, if desired.

YIELD: 6 servings (serving size: about 1 cup).

CALORIES 193; FAT 3g (sat 1g, mono 1g, poly 0.3g); PROTEIN 20g; CARB 20g; FIBER 3.4g; CHOL 40mg; IRON 2mg; SODIUM 825mg; CALC 0mg

RECIPE BENEFIT: low-fat

SOUPS

Beefy Corn and Black Bean Chili

Cheesy Cheddar Corn Bread
Preheat oven to 425°. Combine 2 cups self-rising cornmeal mix (such as White Lily), 1¼ cups nonfat buttermilk, ½ cup reduced-fat sour cream, 1 large egg, lightly beaten, and ½ cup (2 ounces) reduced-fat shredded cheddar cheese in a large bowl. Pour batter into an 8-inch square baking pan coated with butter-flavored cooking spray. Bake at 425° for 20 minutes. Remove from oven; coat top of corn bread with cooking spray. Return to oven; bake 3 minutes or until a wooden pick inserted in center comes out clean and corn bread is golden. Serve warm, or cool completely in pan on a wire rack.

Caldillo

Serve this spicy stew with peeled orange slices sprinkled with cinnamon-sugar. Bottled cinnamon-sugar can be found on the spice aisle of your local supermarket.

Cooking spray
1 pound boneless sirloin steak (about $\frac{1}{2}$ inch thick), cut into bite-sized pieces
1 (8-ounce) container refrigerated prechopped onion
3 cups water
2 ($14\frac{1}{2}$-ounce) cans diced tomatoes with zesty mild green chilies (such as Del Monte), undrained

1 teaspoon ground cumin
3 cups ($\frac{1}{2}$-inch) cubed unpeeled Yukon gold or red potato
$\frac{1}{4}$ cup chopped fresh cilantro (optional)

1. Heat a large Dutch oven coated with cooking spray over high heat. Coat beef with cooking spray, and add to pan. Cook beef 3 minutes; stir in onion. Cook 5 minutes or until liquid evaporates and beef and onion are browned.
2. Stir in 3 cups water, tomatoes, and cumin; cover and bring to a boil. Reduce heat to medium; simmer 20 minutes. Add potato; cover and simmer 10 minutes or until potato is tender. Remove from heat; stir in cilantro, if desired. YIELD: 6 servings (serving size: 1⅓ cups).

CALORIES 165; FAT 3g (sat 1.2g, mono 1.6g, poly 0.2g); PROTEIN 18.3g; CARB 15.5g; FIBER 3.2g; CHOL 28mg; IRON 2mg; SODIUM 595mg; CALC 59mg

RECIPE BENEFIT: low-fat

INGREDIENT TIP: Look for containers of prechopped vegetables in your supermarket's produce section. Or chop the vegetables up to two days ahead, and store them in separate zip-top plastic bags in the refrigerator.

SOUPS

165
calories

Freezing and Thawing

YOU WANT TO MAKE SURE YOU PROPERLY FREEZE FOOD SO IT STILL TASTES GOOD ONCE IT'S THAWED AND REHEATED. To help ensure quality, completely cool a soup or stew before packaging it. You can eliminate freezer burn by using freezer-appropriate containers, such as rigid plastic containers with lids or heavy-duty zip-top plastic bags specifically labeled for freezing. You can prevent ice crystals, which can alter the flavor and texture, by freezing the soup or stew in appropriate-sized containers: Don't allow for much air space in the container, and fill the container almost to the top; if you are using zip-top plastic bags, squeeze out as much air as possible. To thaw, place the frozen soup or stew in the refrigerator to defrost overnight. To prevent the ingredients from becoming mushy, reheat thawed soups and stews over medium-low to medium heat.

SOUPS

Dress Up Soup with Style

1 For casual meals, serve soup right from the pot. Or for casual entertaining, use soup tureens or shiny copper pots.

2 Use your imagination when choosing individual serving bowls. Deep bowls and mugs are good for chunky soups. Wide-rimmed, shallow bowls are ideal for smooth, creamy soups.

3 Consider nontraditional serving dishes such as a cup and saucer for a first-course soup or assorted stemware for a dessert soup.

4 To keep the soup from cooling too quickly, rinse the serving bowls with hot water just before ladling. For chilled soups, place the empty bowls in the refrigerator about 30 minutes before filling.

5 Use simple garnishes, such as lemon or lime wedges or grated, shredded, or shaved cheeses. Sometimes the ingredients used in the recipe can be used to garnish the soup as well as enhancing flavor and texture.

6 If the soup calls for fresh herbs, set aside a few extra sprigs before you begin. You can use the sprigs later as a garnish, or you can chop a little extra to scatter over the soup before serving.

7 For cream or pureed soups, garnish with whole, thinly sliced, or chopped vegetables.

8 A dollop of low-fat sour cream or yogurt can tame the heat and add the finishing touch to a bowl of spicy soup. It can also be swirled into a creamy soup for a decorative presentation.

9 Sprinkle soup with homemade or store-bought croutons or fresh tortillas cut into chips or strips. Or simply lay a breadstick across the rim of the soup bowl.

10 Mound rice or pasta in the center of a bowl (or even off-center), and ladle the soup around it, taking care not to completely cover the rice or pasta.

200
calories

SOUPS

Greens, Beans, and Bacon Soup

This hearty soup, which is chock-full of antioxidants and fiber from the kale and beans, pairs well with a crunchy slice of toasted ciabatta. Look for packages of prechopped kale in the produce section of your supermarket.

3   slices lower-sodium bacon, cut crosswise into ¼-inch pieces
3   cups packed chopped kale
2¼ cups water
1   (15-ounce) can no-salt-added cannellini beans, rinsed and drained

1   (14.5-ounce) can roasted garlic chicken broth
1   cup frozen chopped onion
¼   teaspoon black pepper
Hot sauce (optional)

1. Cook bacon in a large saucepan over medium-high heat 8 minutes or until crisp. Reserve 2 teaspoons drippings in pan; discard excess drippings.
2. Add kale and next 5 ingredients to bacon and drippings in pan. Stir in hot sauce, if desired. Cover and bring to a boil over high heat. Reduce heat, and simmer 25 minutes. Serve immediately. YIELD: 3 servings (serving size: 1⅔ cups).

CALORIES 200; FAT 8.1g (sat 3.3g, mono 3.1g, poly 1.1g); PROTEIN 10.5g; CARB 23.2g; FIBER 5.5g; CHOL 15mg; IRON 2.9mg; SODIUM 792mg; CALC 127mg

KITCHEN TIP: To prepare kale, pull apart the bunch, and examine each leaf. Remove and discard any yellow or limp portions. Wash greens in cool water, agitating with your hands. Replace water two or three times until there are no traces of grit or dirt. Lay kale flat to dry on a dish towel, or use salad spinner to remove excess moisture. Kale leaves often have tough cent veins that need to be removed. Fold the leave in half, slice off the vein, and discard.

Sweet Potato, Leek, and Ham Soup

Prechopped sweet potato is now available in most grocery stores. If you're unable to find it, peel and cube two small sweet potatoes to measure about 3 cups.

Olive oil–flavored cooking spray
1 cup diced cooked ham (such as Cumberland Gap)
1½ cups sliced leek (about 1 large)
2 tablespoons water (optional)
3 cups refrigerated cubed peeled sweet potato (such as Glory)

1 cup fat-free, lower-sodium chicken broth
2 cups water
1 (5-ounce) can evaporated fat-free milk
¼ teaspoon freshly ground black pepper
Thinly sliced leek (optional)
Thinly sliced green onions (optional)

1. Heat a large Dutch oven coated with cooking spray over medium heat. Add ham; cook 3 to 4 minutes or until browned, stirring frequently. Remove ham from pan; set aside.

2. Coat leek with cooking spray, and add to pan; cook, covered, 5 minutes or until leek is very tender, stirring occasionally. Add 2 tablespoons water to pan, if needed, to prevent burning.

3. Add sweet potato and next 4 ingredients, scraping pan to loosen browned bits; bring mixture to a boil. Cover, reduce heat, and simmer 15 minutes or until sweet potato is very tender. Place half of potato mixture in a blender or food processor. Remove center piece of blender lid (to allow steam to escape); secure blender lid on blender. Place a clean towel over opening in blender lid (to avoid splatters). Process until smooth. Pour puree into a large bowl. Repeat procedure with remaining mixture. Return pureed mixture to pan. Stir in ¾ cup reserved ham. Ladle soup into bowls; top servings evenly with remaining ¼ cup reserved ham. Garnish with sliced leek and onions, if desired.

YIELD: 4 servings (serving size: about 1¼ cups).

CALORIES 193; FAT 1g (sat 0.2g, mono 0g, poly 0.1g); PROTEIN 15.5g; CARB 29.2g; FIBER 3.6g; CHOL 26mg; IRON 2mg; SODIUM 625mg; CALC 153mg

RECIPE BENEFIT: low-fat

SOUPS

193
calories

134
calories

Southwestern Chicken and White Bean Soup

We really like the extra zing of flavor from the fresh cilantro. It adds a nice burst of color to the dish as well. Simply toss some of the distinctive herb on top of the soup just before serving.

2 cups shredded cooked chicken breast
1 tablespoon 40%-less-sodium taco seasoning (such as Old El Paso)
Cooking spray
2 (14-ounce) cans fat-free, lower-sodium chicken broth
1 (16-ounce) can cannellini beans or other white beans, rinsed and drained
½ cup green salsa
Light sour cream (optional)
Chopped fresh cilantro (optional)

1. Combine chicken and taco seasoning; toss well to coat. Heat a large saucepan coated with cooking spray over medium-high heat. Add chicken to pan; sauté 2 minutes or until chicken is lightly browned. Add broth, scraping pan to loosen browned bits.

2. Place beans in a small bowl; mash until only a few whole beans remain. Add beans and salsa to pan, stirring well. Bring to a boil. Reduce heat; simmer 10 minutes or until slightly thick. Serve with sour cream and cilantro, if desired.

YIELD: 6 servings (serving size: 1 cup).

CALORIES 134; FAT 3g (sat 0.8g, mono 0.7g, poly 0.5g); PROTEIN 18g; CARB 8.5g; FIBER 1.8g; CHOL 40mg; IRON 1.1mg; SODIUM 623mg; CALC 22mg

RECIPE BENEFIT: low-fat

156
calories

Chicken Pasta Soup

This quick twist on classic chicken noodle soup is loaded with fresh vegetables—carrots, celery, onion, and green bell pepper. You'll agree 100 percent that fresh is best.

Cooking spray

2 (6-ounce) skinless, boneless chicken breasts, cut into bite-sized pieces

1 (8-ounce) container refrigerated prechopped celery, onion, and bell pepper mix

1 cup matchstick-cut carrots

¼ teaspoon freshly ground black pepper

7 cups fat-free, lower-sodium chicken broth

1 cup uncooked whole-wheat rotini (corkscrew pasta)

1. Heat a large Dutch oven coated with cooking spray over medium-high heat. Add chicken and next 3 ingredients to pan; cook 6 minutes or until chicken begins to brown and vegetables are tender, stirring frequently. Add broth; bring to a boil. Add pasta, reduce heat to medium, and cook 8 minutes or until pasta reaches desired degree of doneness. YIELD: 6 servings (serving size: 1½ cups).

CALORIES 156; FAT 3g (sat 0.8g, mono 0.8g, poly 0.4g); PROTEIN 20.4g; CARB 12.8g; FIBER 2.8g; CHOL 40mg; IRON 1.4mg; SODIUM 723mg; CALC 27mg

RECIPE BENEFIT: low-fat

159
calories

Smoked Turkey–Lentil Soup

Throw these ingredients into the slow cooker in the morning, and come home to a hearty and comforting meal without doing any further work. If you prefer to use dried oregano instead of fresh, reduce the amount to ½ teaspoon. Dried herbs are very potent, and a little goes a long way.

6 cups organic vegetable broth
1 (8-ounce) smoked turkey leg
½ pound dried lentils, rinsed and drained
1 (8-ounce) container refrigerated prechopped celery, onion, and bell pepper mix

2 teaspoons chopped fresh oregano
½ teaspoon freshly ground black pepper
Nonfat Greek yogurt (optional)
Oregano sprigs (optional)

1. Place first 6 ingredients in a 3- to 4-quart electric slow cooker. Cover and cook on LOW 8 to 10 hours or until lentils are tender and turkey falls off the bone.
2. Remove turkey leg from cooker. Remove and discard skin. Shred meat; return to cooker, discarding bone. Ladle soup into bowls; garnish with yogurt and oregano sprigs, if desired. YIELD: 8 servings (serving size: 1 cup).

CALORIES 159; FAT 3g (sat 0.9g, mono 1.2g, poly 0.5g); PROTEIN 12.7g; CARB 21.3g; FIBER 5g; CHOL 17mg; IRON 2.2mg; SODIUM 648mg; CALC 26mg

CHOICE INGREDIENT: *Lentils*

Lentils can be found in different sizes and colors, ranging from yellow to red-orange to green and brown, all of which can be purchased whole or split. Lentils cook quickly and don't require soaking, as other dried legumes do. They lend mild, nutty flavor that melds with a wide variety of ingredients.

156
calories

Chicken-Vegetable-Barley Soup

Warm up on a cold winter day with a bowl of this simple and healthful soup. It's rich in fiber, potassium, and magnesium—all of which protect against heart disease. Serve this soup with toasted slices of cheese-topped bâtarde, a small French bread loaf.

5 cups fat-free, lower-sodium chicken broth	1 (16-ounce) package frozen vegetable soup mix with tomatoes
2 cups shredded rotisserie chicken breast	¾ cup quick-cooking barley
½ teaspoon kosher salt	2 cups chopped bagged baby spinach leaves
½ teaspoon freshly ground black pepper	

1. Combine first 5 ingredients in a large Dutch oven. Cover and bring to a boil. Stir in barley; cover, reduce heat, and simmer 10 minutes, stirring occasionally. Remove from heat; stir in spinach, and let stand 5 minutes. YIELD: 8 servings (serving size: about 1 cup).

CALORIES 156; FAT 2.9g (sat 0.8g, mono 1.1g, poly 0.6g); PROTEIN 15.9g; CARB 17.6g; FIBER 3g; CHOL 29mg; IRON 0.8mg; SODIUM 494mg; CALC 11mg

RECIPE BENEFIT: low-fat

MENU • *serves 8*

Chicken-Vegetable-Barley Soup

Garlic Cheddar Toast
Preheat oven to 400°. Combine 1 cup (4 ounces) shredded reduced-fat sharp cheddar cheese, 1 tablespoon light mayonnaise, ½ teaspoon chopped fresh oregano, and 2 minced garlic cloves. Cut 1 (8-ounce) multigrain bâtarde into 16 diagonally-cut slices; top evenly with cheese mixture. Place on a baking sheet. Bake at 400° for 8 minutes or until cheese browns and bread is lightly toasted.

200-CALORIE RECIPES

Desserts

Lemon Pudding Cake

Prepare this recipe in the summertime when you're craving a dessert that's not too heavy. Lemon rind and juice provide tartness, which is balanced by the sweetness of the fresh berries. This dessert is not quite a pudding and not quite a cake—it's something in between. A puddinglike layer forms under the tender cake topping as it bakes. It tastes best when served warm.

1 (9-ounce) package yellow cake mix (such as Jiffy)	Cooking spray
½ cup fat-free milk	⅔ cup boiling water
¼ cup reduced-fat sour cream	2 cups mixed berries
1 lemon	Frozen fat-free whipped topping, thawed (optional)

1. Preheat oven to 350°.

2. Combine first 3 ingredients in a medium bowl. Grate rind, and squeeze juice from lemon to measure 1 teaspoon and 2 tablespoons, respectively. Stir rind and juice into batter just until blended. Spoon batter into an 8-inch square baking dish coated with cooking spray. Pour boiling water over batter (do not stir).

3. Bake at 350° for 28 minutes. Remove from oven; let stand 5 minutes. Spoon cake into 8 individual serving bowls; top with berries and whipped topping, if desired. Serve warm. YIELD: 8 servings (serving size: ⅛ of cake and ¼ cup berries).

CALORIES 168; FAT 3.4g (sat 1g, mono 0.9g, poly 0.9g); PROTEIN 2.4g; CARB 33.2g; FIBER 0.9g; CHOL 3mg; IRON 0.8mg; SODIUM 229mg; CALC 18mg

DESSERTS

136

168 calories

156
calories

White Chocolate–Cherry Rice Pudding

When you're looking for a quick dessert, turn to this superfast pudding that's spiced with ground cinnamon and flecked with cherries. This shortcut method of using an instant pudding mix delivers the characteristic creamy texture of rice pudding without the long cooking time.

3½ cups 1% low-fat milk, divided
⅓ cup dried cherries
2 tablespoons light brown sugar
¼ teaspoon ground cinnamon
1 tablespoon butter
⅛ teaspoon salt
1 cup instant rice
1 (1-ounce) package sugar-free white chocolate instant pudding mix
Cinnamon sticks (optional)

1. Bring 1½ cups milk, dried cherries, and next 4 ingredients to a boil in a medium saucepan over medium heat, stirring occasionally. Stir in rice; cover, and reduce heat to low. Simmer 5 minutes, stirring occasionally.

2. While rice mixture cooks, prepare pudding mix according to package directions using remaining 2 cups milk. Stir prepared pudding into rice mixture. Serve warm. Garnish with cinnamon sticks, if desired. YIELD: 8 servings (serving size: ½ cup).

CALORIES 156; FAT 2.6g (sat 1.6g, mono 0.7g, poly 0.1g); PROTEIN 5g; CARB 27.9g; FIBER 0.7g; CHOL 8mg; IRON 0.9mg; SODIUM 141mg; CALC 142mg

RECIPE BENEFIT: low-fat

Triple-Chocolate Pudding

Modest in appearance yet boasting an intense flavor and a made-from-scratch taste, this simple, satisfying chocolate pudding is the quintessential weeknight dessert. Place plastic wrap on the surface of the hot pudding to prevent a skin from forming during chilling.

1 (5-ounce) package chocolate cook-and-serve pudding mix
1 large egg yolk
4 cups 1% low-fat chocolate milk
1 ounce semisweet chocolate, chopped

1 teaspoon vanilla extract
Frozen reduced-calorie whipped topping, thawed (optional)
Semisweet chocolate shavings (optional)

1. Combine first 3 ingredients in a medium saucepan. Bring to a boil over medium heat, stirring constantly with a whisk. Boil 2 minutes, stirring constantly. Remove from heat. Add chopped chocolate and vanilla, stirring with a whisk until chocolate melts. Cool 5 minutes.

2. Spoon ½ cup pudding into each of 8 individual serving bowls. Serve warm, or cover surface of pudding with plastic wrap, and chill thoroughly. Top each serving with whipped topping, if desired; sprinkle with chocolate shavings, if desired. YIELD: 8 servings (serving size: 1 pudding).

CALORIES 169; FAT 2.8g (sat 1.6g, mono 0.2g, poly 0.1g); PROTEIN 5.2g; CARB 31.3g; FIBER 0.7g; CHOL 31mg; IRON 0.7mg; SODIUM 187mg; CALC 151mg

✳ **RECIPE BENEFIT: low-fat**

169 calories

Lemon-Buttermilk Panna Cotta with Blueberry Sauce

This is a great make-ahead dessert. Running a knife around the edge of each prepared custard makes it easier to remove to a plate.

Panna Cotta:
Cooking spray
1½ tablespoons unflavored gelatin
1 cup whole milk
½ cup plus 2 tablespoons sugar
3 cups low-fat buttermilk
1 teaspoon grated lemon rind

Sauce:
½ cup apple juice
¼ cup sugar
1 tablespoon fresh lemon juice
2 cups blueberries
Mint sprigs (optional)

1. To prepare panna cotta, coat 8 (6-ounce) custard cups with cooking spray. Sprinkle gelatin over whole milk in a small saucepan; let stand 10 minutes. Cook milk mixture over medium-low heat 10 minutes or until gelatin dissolves, stirring constantly with a whisk. Increase heat to medium; add ½ cup plus 2 tablespoons sugar, stirring with a whisk until sugar dissolves. Remove from heat. Add buttermilk and rind, stirring well. Divide mixture evenly among prepared custard cups. Cover and chill at least 5 hours or up to overnight.

2. To prepare sauce, combine apple juice, ¼ cup sugar, and lemon juice in a small saucepan. Bring to a boil over medium-high heat; stir until sugar dissolves. Reduce heat to medium; stir in blueberries. Cook 8 minutes or until blueberries are warm and begin to pop. Cool sauce to room temperature.

3. Place a dessert plate, upside down, on top of each custard cup; invert each panna cotta onto a plate. Serve with sauce. Garnish with mint sprigs, if desired.

YIELD: 8 servings (serving size: 1 panna cotta and about ¼ cup sauce).

CALORIES 173; FAT 2g (sat 1.2g, mono 0.6g, poly 0.1g); PROTEIN 5.4g; CARB 34.8g; FIBER 1g; CHOL 8mg; IRON 0.2mg; SODIUM 117mg; CALC 148mg

DESSERTS

72
calories

Marsala-Poached Figs

This stylish dessert requires little preparation, and you can easily halve or double the recipe to serve fewer or more diners. Give the figs a gentle squeeze to check for their ripeness; they should be quite soft. Serve the figs with toasted pecan halves and small wedges of Gruyère or fontina cheese.

½ cup marsala
1 (3-inch) cinnamon stick
3 black peppercorns

1 tablespoon honey
6 fresh Black Mission figs
(about 8.5 ounces), halved

1. Combine first 4 ingredients in a medium saucepan. Bring to a boil; cook 7 minutes or until syrupy. Add figs; cook 1 minute or until thoroughly heated.
YIELD: 6 servings (serving size: 2 fig halves and about 2 teaspoons sauce).

CALORIES 72; FAT 0g (sat 0g, mono 0g, poly 0g); PROTEIN 0.4g; CARB 13.3g; FIBER 1.2g; CHOL 0mg; IRON 0.2mg; SODIUM 2mg; CALC 15mg

RECIPE BENEFITS: fat-free; low-sodium

CHOICE INGREDIENT: *Figs*

Fresh figs need very little adornment and cooking, thanks to their subtle, sweet flavor and dense texture. For a quick, pleasurable ending to a meal, serve figs raw, or gently simmer them in a sauce for just a few minutes. Figs are available twice a year, with the first crop arriving from June through July, and the second crop coming in early September and lasting through mid-October.

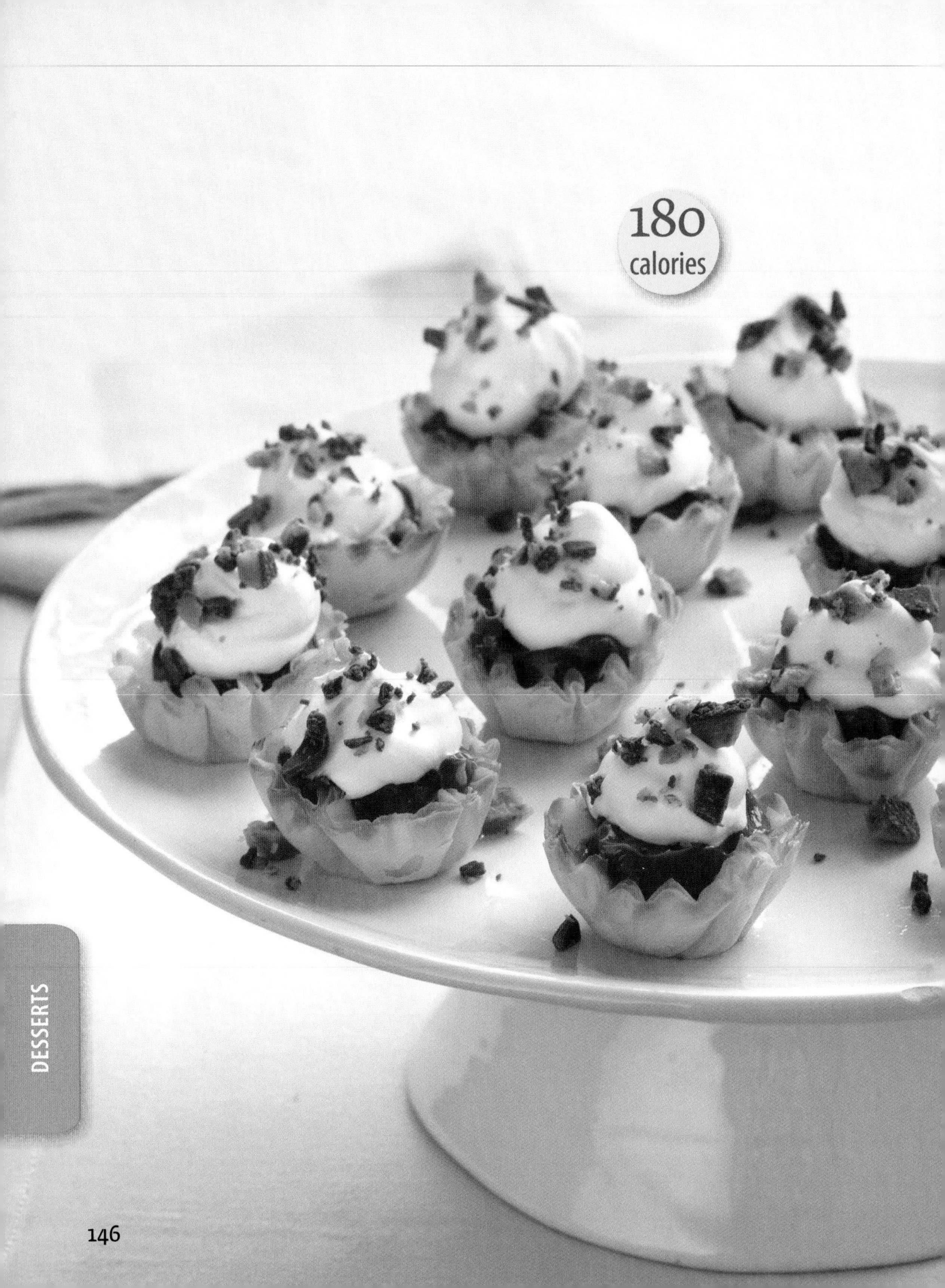
180
calories

Dulce de Leche Tartlets

Looking for a quick dessert that's ideal for a weeknight potluck or party? These petite tarts are the answer. With just the right amount of crunch from the candy bar pieces to complement the rich, smooth dulce de leche filling, they'll disappear fast!

1 (1.9-ounce) package mini phyllo shells (such as Athenos)

⅓ cup canned dulce de leche

1 cup reduced-calorie frozen whipped topping, thawed

1 (1.4-ounce) English toffee candy bar, finely chopped (such as Heath or Skor)

1. Preheat oven to 350°.

2. Arrange phyllo shells on a baking sheet. Bake phyllo shells at 350° for 5 minutes or until crisp. Cool slightly.

3. Spoon about 1 teaspoon dulce de leche into each shell, and top each serving with about 1 tablespoon whipped topping. Sprinkle tartlets evenly with chopped candy. YIELD: 15 servings (serving size: 1 tartlet).

CALORIES 180; FAT 7.7g (sat 2.8g, mono 2.2g, poly 0.6g); PROTEIN 1.3g; CARB 23.4g; FIBER 0.1g; CHOL 14mg; IRON 0.5mg; SODIUM 83mg; CALC 64mg

RECIPE BENEFIT: low-sodium

CHOICE INGREDIENT: *Dulce de Leche*

Dulce de leche, a sweet Spanish sauce, is made by cooking milk and sugar until it reduces to a thick, amber-colored syrup. Preparing homemade dulce de leche can take up to 3 hours; for quick weeknight cooking, we recommend purchasing a can at your supermarket or a Latin market. Look for dulce de leche alongside the canned milks. Since it is similar in flavor and texture to caramel, you can substitute caramel sauce.

Blueberry-Lemon Cream Parfaits

In these parfaits, lemon curd combined with cream cheese and ice cream forms a custardlike sauce. Substitute sliced strawberries for the blueberries, or use both for a variation.

¼ cup (2 ounces) block-style ⅓-less-fat cream cheese
2 tablespoons lemon curd
¾ cup vanilla light ice cream, slightly softened (such as Edy's)
1 teaspoon grated lemon rind
½ cup coarsely crushed sugar-free shortbread cookies (about 12 cookies; such as Murray's)
1 cup blueberries

1. Place cream cheese and lemon curd in a small bowl; beat with a mixer at medium-high speed until smooth. Add ice cream and lemon rind; beat well.

2. Spoon 1 tablespoon cookie crumbs into each of 4 glasses. Top each with 2 tablespoons cream cheese mixture and 2 tablespoons blueberries. Repeat procedure once. Serve immediately. YIELD: 4 servings (serving size: 1 parfait).

CALORIES 183; FAT 7.1g (sat 3.6g, mono 2.7, poly 0.6); PROTEIN 3.7g; CARB 27.7g; FIBER 2.4g; CHOL 24.3mg; IRON 0.4mg; SODIUM 142mg; CALC 53mg

183
calories

Fresh Pineapple-Lime Dessert Salsa

Crystallized ginger contributes to the sweet and spicy notes of this pineapple salsa. Look for it in the Asian-food section of your supermarket. Try the salsa spooned over ½ cup blood orange or strawberry sorbet or light vanilla ice cream.

2	cups chopped fresh pineapple	2	teaspoons grated fresh lime rind
1½	tablespoons chopped fresh mint	1½	tablespoons fresh lime juice
1½	tablespoons honey		Blood orange sorbet (optional)
2	teaspoons chopped crystallized ginger		Fresh mint sprigs (optional)

1. Combine pineapple and next 5 ingredients in a medium bowl; let stand 10 minutes to develop juices. Spoon each serving over sorbet, and garnish with mint, if desired. YIELD: 8 servings (serving size: ¼ cup salsa).

CALORIES 37; FAT 0.1g (sat 0g, mono 0g, poly 0g); PROTEIN 0.3g; CARB 9.9g; FIBER 0.5g; CHOL 0mg; IRON 0.3mg; SODIUM 1mg; CALC 8mg

RECIPE BENEFITS: fat-free; low-sodium

KITCHEN TIP: To easily slice a pineapple, a sharp chef's knife is key. Lay the pineapple horizontally on a cutting board, and cut off the leafy top (the plume) and the base. Stand the pineapple upright on the cutting board; cut down the sides to remove the rind. Remove as little of the flesh as possible. While the pineapple is upright, cut it into thirds by carefully slicing downward to remove the fibrous core. Discard the core.

DESSERTS

37
calories

128 calories

Coconut-Oat Cookies

1¼ cups all-purpose flour

1 cup old-fashioned rolled oats

¾ cup packed dark brown sugar

1 teaspoon baking soda

⅛ teaspoon salt

¼ cup chilled butter, cut into small pieces

¾ cup flaked sweetened coconut

¼ cup water

2 tablespoons light corn syrup

Cooking spray

1. Preheat oven to 350°.

2. Lightly spoon flour into dry measuring cups; level with a knife. Combine flour and next 4 ingredients in a medium bowl. Cut in butter with a pastry blender or 2 knives until mixture resembles coarse meal. Stir in coconut. Add water and corn syrup; stir just until dry ingredients are moist.

3. Turn dough out onto a lightly floured surface; knead 2 or 3 times. Roll dough to ½-inch thickness; cut with a 2½-inch cookie cutter. Reroll trimmings to make additional cookies.

4. Place cookies on a baking sheet coated with cooking spray. Bake at 350° for 17 minutes or until lightly browned. Cool on pan 5 minutes. Transfer to a wire rack to cool completely. YIELD: 16 cookies (serving size: 1 cookie).

CALORIES 128; FAT 4.3g (sat 2.8g, mono 1g, poly 0.3g); PROTEIN 1.8g; CARB 21.2g; FIBER 1.1g; CHOL 8mg; IRON 0.9mg; SODIUM 131mg; CALC 11mg

RECIPE BENEFIT: low-sodium

How to Make Great Low-Fat Cookies

Ingredients

USE THE EXACT INGREDIENTS CALLED FOR IN THE RECIPE. BAKING COOKIES IS LIKE CONDUCTING A SCIENCE EXPERIMENT—THE RIGHT BALANCE AND TYPE OF INGREDIENTS IS CRUCIAL.

• Don't replace butter with diet margarine or tub-style spread. These have too much water and too little fat to produce the right results.

• We generally don't recommend using sugar substitutes in baking. Sugar helps keep cookies moist and soft; it also enriches the flavor as sugar caramelizes.

• Measure flour correctly; too much flour will make cookies tough.

• If the batter seems dry, don't add more liquid. This makes for a cakelike cookie that spreads too much.

• Don't use egg substitutes unless the recipe calls for it. The yolk of the egg helps disperse the fat, keeping the cookie tender and moist.

Pans

FOR EVEN BAKING, USE A HEAVY BAKING OR COOKIE SHEET (WHICH HAS A LIP ON ONE OR BOTH ENDS). A LARGER BAKING SHEET (17 X 14 INCHES) ALLOWS YOU TO BAKE MORE COOKIES AT A TIME THAN A STANDARD 15 X 12–INCH PAN.

• Nonstick baking sheets tend to make the cookies too dark on the bottom. We prefer silver-colored aluminum pans.

• The air-cushioned pans work fine, but they're not necessarily better than good-quality heavy baking sheets. And you can't put the air-cushioned pans in the dishwasher.

• Be sure to bake cookies in the correct size pan; otherwise, the baking time and texture of the cookie will vary.

Baking

COOKIES BAKE MORE EVENLY WHEN THEY'RE ABOUT THE SAME SIZE. WHEN THE RECIPE SAYS TO "DROP BY LEVEL TABLESPOONS," USE A MEASURING SPOON, NOT A TABLEWARE SPOON. AND DON'T FORGET COOKIES NEED PLENTY OF SPACE BETWEEN THEM TO ALLOW FOR SPREADING.

• Bake cookies in an oven that has been preheated for 15 minutes.
• Place the rack in the second position from the bottom of the oven so there is room for air to circulate on all sides of the baking sheet.
• Check for doneness at the earliest time to prevent overbaking. Opening and closing the oven door often can change the baking time.
• Let the baking sheet cool completely between baking batches of cookies.
• Cool bar cookies completely in the pan before cutting into bars to help ensure you get a nice "clean" cut.

Storing and Freezing

YOU CAN FREEZE MOST COOKIE DOUGH AND BAKED COOKIES UP TO SIX MONTHS.

• Use an airtight container to store soft, chewy cookies and bars.
• If the cookie has a glaze on top, use wax paper between layers to keep the cookies from sticking together.
• Store bar cookies in the pan in which they were baked—simply seal them tightly with aluminum foil or plastic wrap.
• Place crisp cookies in a jar with a loose-fitting lid.

Chocolate Peanut Butter Cookies

This simple mix-and-drop dough comes together in minutes.

1 cup granulated sugar	1 large egg
1 cup packed brown sugar	2⅔ cups all-purpose flour (about 12 ounces)
½ cup creamy peanut butter	1 teaspoon baking powder
¼ cup water	1 teaspoon baking soda
¼ cup canola oil	½ teaspoon salt
2 teaspoons vanilla extract	⅔ cup semisweet chocolate minichips
2 large egg whites	

1. Preheat oven to 350°.

2. Combine first 8 ingredients in a large bowl; beat with a mixer at medium speed until smooth.

3. Lightly spoon flour into dry measuring cups; level with a knife. Combine flour and next 3 ingredients in a small bowl; stir with a whisk. Add flour mixture to peanut butter mixture, stirring just until combined. Stir in minichips. Drop dough by tablespoonfuls 2 inches apart on 2 baking sheets. Bake at 350° for 12 minutes or until golden. Cool on a wire rack. YIELD: 3 dozen (serving size: 1 cookie).

CALORIES 128; FAT 4.5g (sat 1.1g, mono 2.2g, poly 1g); PROTEIN 2.3g; CARB 20.5g; FIBER 0.6g; CHOL 6mg; IRON 0.8mg; SODIUM 106mg; CALC 16mg

✳ **RECIPE BENEFIT: low-sodium**

128 calories

89 calories

DESSERTS

Lemon-Honey Drop Cookies

You can make these citrusy cookies with orange rind and orange juice instead of lemon.

$1/2$ cup granulated sugar
7 tablespoons butter, softened
2 teaspoons grated lemon rind
$1/3$ cup honey
$1/2$ teaspoon lemon extract
1 large egg
$1^{3}/_{4}$ cups all-purpose flour

1 teaspoon baking powder
$1/2$ teaspoon salt
$1/4$ cup plain fat-free yogurt
Cooking spray
1 cup powdered sugar
2 tablespoons fresh lemon juice
2 teaspoons grated lemon rind

1. Preheat oven to 350°.

2. Beat first 3 ingredients with a mixer at medium speed until light and fluffy. Add honey, extract, and egg; beat until well blended. Lightly spoon flour into dry measuring cups; level with a knife. Combine flour, baking powder, and salt, stirring well with a whisk. Add flour mixture to sugar mixture alternately with yogurt, beginning and ending with flour mixture. Drop by level tablespoons 2 inches apart onto baking sheets coated with cooking spray. Bake at 350° for 12 minutes or until lightly browned.

3. Combine powdered sugar and juice in a small bowl; stir with a whisk. Brush powdered sugar mixture evenly over warm cookies. Sprinkle evenly with 2 teaspoons rind. Remove cookies from pans; cool on wire racks. YIELD: 32 cookies (serving size: 1 cookie).

CALORIES 89; FAT 2.8g (sat 1.6g, mono 0.8g, poly 0.2g); PROTEIN 1.1g; CARB 15.3g; FIBER 0.2g; CHOL 14mg; IRON 0.4mg; SODIUM 81mg; CALC 15mg

RECIPE BENEFITS: low-fat; low sodium

> **KITCHEN TIP:** Several things can cause your cookies to burn on the bottom—dark cookie sheets, for one. If your pans are dark, decrease your oven temperature by 25°. Make sure the oven rack is in the second position from the bottom of the oven, and bake only one sheet of cookies at a time to ensure proper air circulation. Finally, check your oven temperature periodically with an oven thermometer. Many ovens have hot spots or heat to a temperature higher than they are set for. If the temperature is inaccurate, adjust the dial accordingly.

Strawberry Frozen Yogurt

Fresh thyme may seem like an unusual ingredient in a dessert, but in this recipe, it adds a delicate herb flavor that complements the sweet strawberries.

- 8 cups strawberries, halved
- ¼ cup packed brown sugar
- 2 fresh thyme sprigs (optional)
- 10 tablespoons granulated sugar
- ¼ cup water
- 1 tablespoon fresh lemon juice
- Dash of salt
- 1 (17.6-ounce) carton plain fat-free Greek yogurt
- 1 tablespoon vanilla extract
- Fresh thyme sprigs (optional)

1. Place strawberries, brown sugar, and, if desired, thyme in a medium saucepan. Cook over medium-low heat 20 minutes or until strawberries begin to fall apart. Remove from heat; remove and discard thyme sprigs.

2. While strawberries cook, combine granulated sugar and next 3 ingredients in a small saucepan. Bring to a boil; boil 1 to 2 minutes or until sugar dissolves. Stir syrup into cooked strawberry mixture. Cool 1 hour.

3. Process half of strawberry mixture in batches in a blender until puréed. Pour pureed strawberry mixture into the freezer can of a 3-quart ice-cream freezer. Repeat procedure with remaining strawberry mixture. Add yogurt and vanilla to ice-cream freezer, stirring well with a whisk. Freeze according to manufacturer's instructions. Spoon into a freezer-safe container. Cover and freeze until firm. Garnish with thyme sprigs, if desired. YIELD: 16 servings (serving size: ½ cup).

CALORIES 85; FAT 0.2g (sat 0g, mono 0g, poly 0.1g); PROTEIN 3.2g; CARB 18.1g; FIBER 1.4g; CHOL 0mg; IRON 0.4mg; SODIUM 23mg; CALC 35mg

RECIPE BENEFITS: fat-free; low-sodium

DESSERTS

85
calories

All in the Gelato Family

Gelato (jeh-LAH-toh)—which comes from gelare, the Italian word for "to freeze"—is the umbrella term for any frozen Italian dessert.

GRANITA (GRAH-NEE-TAH)—A fruit-based gelato, it has a decidedly different texture from that of gelato or sorbetto. Because it's frozen and then scraped to form coarse ice granules, granita is slushy.

GELATO—In addition to its more general definition, it also refers to a milk-based concoction with a dense, buttery consistency similar to that of American ice cream. You can serve it in an ice-cream cone.

SORBETTO (SOR-BAY-TOH)—This fruit-based gelato doesn't contain any dairy products. You may know it better as sorbet.

Chambord Granita

This refreshing frozen treat received our Test Kitchens' highest rating.

105 calories

3 **cups water, divided**	4 **cups fresh raspberries**
1 **cup sugar**	1 **cup Chambord (raspberry-flavored liqueur)**

1. Combine 1 cup water and sugar in a saucepan; bring to a boil, stirring until sugar dissolves. Remove from heat; cool completely.

2. Place raspberries in a blender, and process until smooth. Press raspberry puree through a sieve into a medium bowl, and discard seeds. Stir in sugar syrup, 2 cups water, and liqueur. Pour into an 11 x 7–inch baking dish. Cover; freeze 8 hours or until firm.

3. Remove mixture from freezer; let stand 10 minutes. Scrape with a fork until fluffy. YIELD: 16 servings (serving size: ½ cup).

CALORIES 105; FAT 0.2g (sat 0g, mono 0g, poly 0.1g); PROTEIN 0.3g; CARB 21.3g; FIBER 0g; CHOL 0mg; IRON 0.2mg; SODIUM 0mg; CALC 7mg

RECIPE BENEFITS: fat-free; low-sodium

Pineapple Sorbet

If you don't have an ice-cream freezer, use a covered metal bowl. Freeze the mixture three hours or until it's hard on the outside but slushy in the middle. Remove it from the freezer, beat with a whisk until smooth, cover it, and freeze for four hours or until sorbet is firm.

116 calories

1 **small pineapple, peeled and cored**	1 **cup plus 2 tablespoons sugar**
2 **tablespoons fresh lemon juice**	**Mint sprigs (optional)**

1. Cut pineapple into 2-inch pieces. Place pineapple and lemon juice in a food processor; process until smooth. Add sugar; process 1 minute or until sugar dissolves.

2. Pour mixture into freezer can of an ice-cream freezer; freeze according to manufacturer's instructions. Spoon sorbet into a freezer-safe container; cover and freeze 1 hour or until firm. Garnish with mint sprigs, if desired. YIELD: 9 servings (serving size: ½ cup).

CALORIES 116; FAT 0.2g (sat 0g, mono 0.1g, poly 0.1g); PROTEIN 0.2g; CARB 30g; FIBER 0.5g; CHOL 0mg; IRON 0.2mg; SODIUM 1mg; CALC 3mg

Bittersweet Chocolate Sorbet

190 calories

Freeze the sorbet up to two days in advance; let it stand at room temperature 15 minutes to soften before scooping.

2½ cups water
1¼ cups sugar
½ cup unsweetened cocoa

3 ounces bittersweet chocolate, finely chopped
2 teaspoons vanilla extract

1. Bring water to a boil in a medium saucepan. Stir in sugar and cocoa; reduce heat, and simmer 5 minutes, stirring frequently. Remove from heat; add chocolate and vanilla, stirring until chocolate melts. Cover and chill completely.

2. Pour chocolate mixture into freezer can of an ice-cream freezer; freeze according to manufacturer's instructions. Spoon sorbet into a freezer-safe container; cover and freeze 1 hour or until firm. YIELD: 6 servings (serving size: about ⅔ cup).

CALORIES 190; FAT 5.3g (sat 3.2g, mono 0.9g, poly 0.1g); PROTEIN 1.8g; CARB 39.6g; FIBER 2.6g; CHOL 0mg; IRON 1.1mg; SODIUM 2mg; CALC 8mg

RECIPE BENEFIT: low-sodium

Strawberry-Buttermilk Gelato

134 calories

2 cups sugar
2 cups water

5 cups quartered strawberries (about 4 pints)
2 cups low-fat buttermilk

1. Combine sugar and water in a large saucepan; bring to a boil, stirring until sugar dissolves. Pour into a large bowl; cool completely.

2. Place strawberries in a blender; process until smooth. Add strawberry puree and buttermilk to sugar syrup; stir to combine.

3. Pour strawberry mixture into freezer can of an ice-cream freezer, and freeze according to manufacturer's instructions. Spoon gelato into a freezer-safe container; cover and freeze 1 hour or until firm. YIELD: 16 servings (serving size: ½ cup).

CALORIES 134; FAT 0.8g (sat 0.3g, mono 0.2g, poly 0.1g); PROTEIN 1.6g; CARB 31.7g; FIBER 1.7g; CHOL 1mg; IRON 0.3mg; SODIUM 17mg; CALC 48mg

DESSERTS

Nutritional Analysis

How to Use It and Why Glance at the end of any *Cooking Light* recipe, and you'll see how committed we are to helping you make the best of today's light cooking. With chefs, registered dietitians, home economists, and a computer system that analyzes every ingredient, *Cooking Light* gives you authoritative dietary detail like no other magazine. We go to such lengths so you can see how our recipes fit into your healthful eating plan. If you're trying to lose weight, the calorie and fat figures will probably help most. But if you're keeping a close eye on the sodium, cholesterol, and saturated fat in your diet, we provide those numbers, too. And because many women don't get enough iron or calcium, we can help there, as well. Finally, there's a fiber analysis for those of us who don't get enough roughage.

Here's a helpful guide to put our nutritional analysis numbers into perspective. Remember, one size doesn't fit all, so take your lifestyle, age, and circumstances into consideration when determining your nutrition needs. For example, pregnant or breast-feeding women need more protein, calories, and calcium. And men older than 50 need 1,200mg of calcium daily, 200mg more than the amount recommended for younger men.

In Our Nutritional Analysis, We Use These Abbreviations

sat	saturated fat	**CHOL**	cholesterol
mono	monounsaturated fat	**CALC**	calcium
poly	polyunsaturated fat	**g**	gram
CARB	carbohydrates	**mg**	milligram

Daily Nutrition Guide

	Women Ages 25 to 50	Women over 50	Men over 24
Calories	2,000	2,000 or less	2,700
Protein	50g	50g or less	63g
Fat	65g or less	65g or less	88g or less
Saturated Fat	20g or less	20g or less	27g or less
Carbohydrates	304g	304g	410g
Fiber	25g to 35g	25g to 35g	25g to 35g
Cholesterol	300mg or less	300mg or less	300mg or less
Iron	18mg	8mg	8mg
Sodium	2,300mg or less	1,500mg or less	2,300mg or less
Calcium	1,000mg	1,200mg	1,000mg

Metric Equivalents

The information in the following charts is provided to help cooks outside the United States successfully use the recipes in this book. All equivalents are approximate.

Cooking/Oven Temperatures

	Fahrenheit	Celsius	Gas Mark
Freeze Water	32° F	0° C	
Room Temperature	68° F	20° C	
Boil Water	212° F	100° C	
Bake	325° F	160° C	3
	350° F	180° C	4
	375° F	190° C	5
	400° F	200° C	6
	425° F	220° C	7
	450° F	230° C	8
Broil			Grill

Liquid Ingredients by Volume

¼ tsp	=	1 ml			
½ tsp	=	2 ml			
1 tsp	=	5 ml			
3 tsp	= 1 tbl	= ½ floz	=	15 ml
2 tbls	= ⅛ cup	= 1 floz	=	30 ml
4 tbls	= ¼ cup	= 2 floz	=	60 ml
5⅓ tbls	= ⅓ cup	= 3 floz	=	80 ml
8 tbls	= ½ cup	= 4 floz	=	120 ml
10⅔ tbls	= ⅔ cup	= 5 floz	=	160 ml
12 tbls	= ¾ cup	= 6 floz	=	180 ml
16 tbls	= 1 cup	= 8 floz	=	240 ml
1 pt	= 2 cups	= 16 floz	=	480 ml
1 qt	= 4 cups	= 32 floz	=	960 ml
	33 fl oz=1000 ml	= 1l		

Dry Ingredients by Weight

(To convert ounces to grams, multiply the number of ounces by 30.)

1 oz	=	¹⁄₁₆ lb	=	30 g
4 oz	=	¼ lb	=	120 g
8 oz	=	½ lb	=	240 g
12 oz	=	¾ lb	=	360 g
16 oz	=	1 lb	=	480 g

Length

(To convert inches to centimeters, multiply the number of inches by 2.5.)

1 in =		2.5 cm
6 in =	½ ft	= 15 cm
12 in =	1 ft	= 30 cm
36 in =	3 ft = 1 yd =	90 cm
40 in =		100 cm = 1m

Equivalents for Different Types of Ingredients

Standard Cup	Fine Powder (ex. flour)	Grain (ex. rice)	Granular (ex. sugar)	Liquid Solids (ex. butter)	Liquid (ex. milk)
1	140 g	150 g	190 g	200 g	240 ml
¾	105 g	113 g	143 g	150 g	180 ml
⅔	93 g	100 g	125 g	133 g	160 ml
½	70 g	75 g	95 g	100 g	120 ml
⅓	47 g	50 g	63 g	67 g	80 ml
¼	35 g	38 g	48 g	50 g	60 ml
⅛	18 g	19 g	24 g	25 g	30 ml

Index

Chicken BLT Salad with Creamy Avocado–Horned
   Melon Dressing, 89
*Chicken Salad with Asparagus and Creamy Dill
   Dressing, 97
Chicken, Spinach, and Blueberry Salad with
   Pomegranate Vinaigrette, 95
Citrus Vinaigrette, 101
*Feta-Chicken Couscous Salad with Basil, 99
*Greek Salad Bowl, 90
Heirloom Tomato and Goat Cheese Salad with
   Bacon Dressing, 86
Honeyed Lemon-Dijon Vinaigrette, 100
*Mediterranean Tuna Salad, 72
Poppy Seed Dressing, 100
*Spinach Salad with Grilled Pork Tenderloin
   and Nectarines, 82
Steak Salad with Creamy Horseradish
   Dressing, 81
Taco Salad with Cilantro-Lime Vinaigrette, 75
*Yucatecan Rice Salad, 78

SANDWICHES
Gruyère-Thyme Grilled Cheese Sandwiches, 115

SIDES
Cheesy Cheddar Corn Bread, 117
Garlic Cheddar Toast, 133
Ginger-Roasted Green Beans, 65
Greek-Style Pita Chips, 72
Herb-Crusted Broiled Tomatoes, 55

Orange and Radish Cabbage Slaw, 46
Roasted Zucchini, 67
Sautéed Corn and Cherry Tomatoes, 42
Sesame Wonton Crisps, 106
Sweet Pea and Fresh Mint Couscous, 58

SOUPS
*Beefy Corn and Black Bean Chili, 116
*Caldillo, 118
*Cheese Tortellini and Vegetable Soup, 113
*Chicken Pasta Soup, 129
*Chicken-Vegetable-Barley Soup, 133
*French Onion Soup, 115
*Greens, Beans, and Bacon Soup, 123
New England Clam Chowder, 109
Oriental Soup with Mushrooms, Bok Choy,
   and Shrimp, 106
*Smoked Turkey–Lentil Soup, 131
Smoky Black Bean Soup with Avocado-Lime
   Salsa, 110
*Southwestern Chicken and White Bean
   Soup, 127
*Sweet Potato, Leek, and Ham Soup, 124
*Thai Coconut Shrimp Soup, 104

VEGETARIAN
Mediterranean-Style Frittata, 55
*Sautéed Vegetables and Spicy Tofu, 52

* quick & easy   * make ahead